THE COLLECTED COURSES OF THE ACADEMY OF EUROPEAN LAW

Volume XXVI/2

What's Left of the Law of Integration?
Decay and Resistance in European Union Law

THE COLLECTED COURSES OF THE ACADEMY OF EUROPEAN LAW

Edited by
Professor Nehal Bhuta,
Professor Claire Kilpatrick,
and Professor Joanne Scott

Assistant Editor
Anny Bremner

Each year the Academy of European Law in Florence, Italy, invites a group of outstanding lecturers to teach at its summer courses on Human Rights law and the European Union. A 'general course' is given in each of the two fields by a distinguished scholar or practitioner, who examines the field as a whole through a particular thematic, conceptual, or philosophical lens, or looks at a theme in the context of the overall body of law. In addition, a series of 'specialized courses' brings together a group of highly qualified scholars to explore and analyse a specific theme in relation to Human Rights law and EU law. The Academy's mission, to produce scholarly analyses which are at the cutting edge of the two fields, is achieved through publication of this series, the Collected Courses of the Academy of European Law.

WHAT'S LEFT OF THE LAW OF INTEGRATION?

DECAY AND RESISTANCE IN EUROPEAN UNION LAW

JULIO BAQUERO CRUZ

OXFORD
UNIVERSITY PRESS

OXFORD
UNIVERSITY PRESS

Great Clarendon Street, Oxford, OX2 6DP,
United Kingdom

Oxford University Press is a department of the University of Oxford.
It furthers the University's objective of excellence in research, scholarship,
and education by publishing worldwide. Oxford is a registered trade mark of
Oxford University Press in the UK and in certain other countries

First Edition published in 2018

Published in the United States of America by Oxford University Press
198 Madison Avenue, New York, NY 10016, United States of America

British Library Cataloguing in Publication Data
Data available

Library of Congress Control Number: 2018941856

ISBN 978–0–19–883061–0 (hbk)
ISBN 978–0–19–883409–0 (pbk)

PREFACE

At some point in the autumn of 2014, Marise Cremona and Loïc Azoulai invited me to give the general course on Union law at the 2015 session of the Academy of European Law at the European University Institute. I was a researcher at the Institute from 1997 to 2000. Two of the summers in between I stayed in Florence in July to attend the lectures of the Academy. I remember listening to Joseph Weiler, Paul Craig, Neil MacCormick, Matthias Kumm, and some others. I also recall the exciting experience of the courses, surrounded by many gifted young people, in the midst of a vivid intellectual exchange. The proposal made me feel honoured and proud, but it also worried me. Seeing the names and stature of my predecessors, I feared not being quite up to the task. Being so busy between work, teaching, and family duties, I also feared not having enough time to prepare properly. In the end, however, the wish to share my ideas with a group of students prevailed, and I accepted.

I proposed the title which this book bears: *What's left of the law of integration?* My intention was to discuss the impact of the difficult situation the European Union is currently going through on some structural elements of its legal order, looking for symptoms of decay, exploring examples of resistance, and assessing its overall state of health. I also wanted to put the original choices made by the drafters of the Treaties and by the Court of Justice in their proper historical perspective, understanding Union law as a tool of civilization, and explaining its current decline, at least in part, as a consequence of the waning of the initial impetus behind integration. The concrete themes to be explored were the following: primacy, the national resistance to it and constitutional pluralism; the preliminary rulings procedure; Union citizenship, equality, and human dignity; the scope of the Charter and the standard of protection of fundamental rights; and the rigidity and fragmentation of the Union system in connection with the recent occasional use of international law as an alternative to Union law. My idea was to look at the development of the law throughout the decades, inevitably losing much detail, but hopefully also uncovering structural connections and continuities. This guided the choice of texts and the questions sent to the students to read and analyse before each class.

The course took place between 2 and 9 July 2015. I have fond memories of the lectures, in which I probably received more from the students than I gave to them. They were an ideal audience and interlocutor: a group of brilliant young jurists, not stuck in national legal conceptions, always asking the crucial and most difficult questions, ready to search for a deeper understanding of the issues discussed. Many of the classes went on beyond the planned schedule and sometimes the conversation continued over lunch or coffee. The exchanges with the organizers and with other people teaching at the Academy or present in Florence during that period, including David Anderson, Alberto Alemanno, Stéphanie Francq, Amandine Garde, Hans Micklitz, and Bruno de Witte, and the hours spent reading and thinking in the quiet and shady garden of Pensione Bencistà, were also very enriching.

I left Florence with a pile of annotated texts, the detailed outlines for each class, a long document with notes and issues to explore, an unrealistically long list of things to read, and a rough structure for the book to come. Back in Brussels, I found myself immersed in an increasing volume of work and responsibility, never having the kind of time and energy I would have liked to devote to this book—in particular, to engage more fully with the ever-growing academic literature. I thought, nevertheless, that there might be some value in putting the ideas of the course in writing, however imperfect it would be. Finishing this book has taken me a long time, not least because its subject continued to evolve while I was working on it.

The reader will understand that the ideas presented here are strictly personal and may not be attributed to the Commission or its Legal Service. I have developed them while studying, practising, and teaching Union law over a fairly long period of time. My practical work has always been accompanied by a parallel theoretical effort: not only doing things, but also thinking about the wider implications of what one does.

Thanks are due to Julian Currall and Jonathan Tomkin for comments and a thorough revision of chapters 2 and 3; to

Giuseppe Martinico for various comments and advice; to Agustín Menéndez, Erik Eriksen, and John Erik Fossum, for inviting me to ARENA in Oslo to discuss constitutional pluralism with Neil Walker in April 2015, giving me a first chance to explore some of the ideas presented in chapter 3; to Hannes Kraemer for comments on chapter 6; to Bernardo Cortese, for inviting me to participate in the examining board of the Ph.D. thesis written by Eleonora Paggi on differentiated integration, held in Padova on 2 November 2017, which allowed me to think further about the themes of chapter 7; to the students of the general course on Union law at Sciences Po in Paris, with whom I had productive exchanges on some of the subjects of this book; to Anny Bremner for her kind help during the course and in connection with the publication of this book; to Carlos Simón, for recovering a lost file which contained two months of work; and to Ceri Warner, for her very valuable copy editing.

Julio Baquero Cruz
Brussels, March 2018

CONTENTS

1

SOME THINGS PIERRE PESCATORE TOLD ME

In the beginning of 2001, shortly after arriving to Luxembourg to start working at the chambers of Gil Carlos Rodríguez Iglesias, then president of the European Court of Justice, I called Pierre Pescatore, who was one of the negotiators of the Treaty of Rome, a former judge of the Court, a fine legal scholar, and a central figure in the development of Community law. I had read his writings during my studies and for my doctoral research, and the close affinity I felt with his ideas and general approach made me want to meet him in person. Pescatore received me, we started talking, and during the four years I spent in the Grand Duchy we often met to discuss the past, present, and future of integration and its law.

We had fascinating conversations that invited me to think about the contemporary development of Union law as the continuation of a movement which had started many decades before, for very grave reasons that could give it a different and more dense meaning. His very presence and authority prompted me to think about Union law not only logically, as people usually do, but also chronologically, paying attention to its slow 'geological' development and historical significance.

In our meetings, which sometimes had a precise agenda, such as discussing this or that recent judgment, the ongoing activities of the European Convention, an academic article, or a book of legal theory, but which could also move very quickly from law to literature to history or philosophy, we always had a completely free exchange of ideas. Pescatore talked a lot, but he also listened carefully, engaged in discussion, and could hesitate and change his mind. He had a keen interest in the news that I, in my late twenties, could bring him from the Court, and also in my opinions about the state of European affairs.

What's Left of the Law of Integration? Decay and Resistance in European Union Law.
First Edition. Julio Baquero Cruz. Published 2018 by Oxford University Press.

Among the many things Pescatore told me, I would like to recall three which have been important for the approach I try to follow in legal work, both theoretical and practical, and which have also guided some of the thoughts presented in this book.

The first one is a story about how the physical copy of the Treaty of Rome, which was to be signed on 25 March 1957 in a formal ceremony at the Campidoglio, was not ready because of a delay at the *Zecca dello Stato*, the Italian state printing works. What the representatives of the six Member States ended up signing was a stack of white pages, with the first printed pages on top.

'Vous voyez?' Pescatore added. He didn't need to say more for me to understand that the story was a telling metaphor of the journey to an unknown (or not totally known) destination, which those states (and their peoples) had decided to start for reasons they understood very well, and which many other states were to join later on. In spite of its economic object, the Treaty of Rome was very different from the traditional one-off commercial international instrument with detailed clauses, specific commitments, and a lean or non-existent institutional structure. The representatives of the six states knew that they were signing a much more ambitious framework agreement which included broad and open-textured provisions and a sophisticated institutional system which could produce 'secondary law' and case law, fill in the empty spaces of that agreement, and unfold following its own logic.

A second thing that I would like to recall was his experience of *satori* in the 1960s, when, while visiting the MoMA in New York, he discovered one of the kinetic works of Alexander Calder, known as 'mobiles'. As he watched that group of elements and wires moving freely in the air he understood that the system of integration was also a 'mobile', a structure of institutional actors, powers, procedures, norms, principles, and values, always in equilibrium but never achieving a lasting stable position—a sort of *perpetuum mobile*, in constant evolution as a result of its productive interactions. Pescatore also recognized it as an integrated system in which whenever something is touched at any level, that single and sometimes almost imperceptible touch has consequences for all the other levels. And, finally, he realized that in that system the legal element is closely linked to, and sometimes in deep tension with, the underlying institutional structure.

The Community was a mobile, not a solid piece of stone with a more or less readable inscription entrusted to high priests to be worshipped by an eternal political community. It was a light and complex mobile, and one in which 'chance', unexpected chain reactions and unprecedented structural constellations played a large role. It was very interesting to hear those words from the reporting judge of *Simmenthal*, *ERTA* and Opinion 1/78,[1] one of the minds behind Article 177 of the Treaty establishing the European Economic Community (the original provision on the preliminary rulings procedure), and the author of an essay about how the Court could counter the inaction or paralysis of the legislature by acting as a catalyst.[2] I already knew that the people who drafted the Treaties of Paris and Rome and conceived the foundational case law had brilliant technical skills—our best drafting efforts seeming so clumsy when compared with their clear texts. This made me realize, in addition, that they were inspired by higher ideals and had a keen awareness of the implications of what they were doing.

A third thing I remember from Pescatore is the strong emphasis he always put on the notion of integration and of Community law as a 'law of integration'. This latter expression, which he coined, still captures the essence of the legal system that is now called European Union law. It conveys the idea of the law of an open process and not of a solid state—or 'constitution'—to be reflected and perpetuated by the legal order. This expression was used by Pescatore in the eponymous book which contained a series of lectures he gave in Geneva in 1971, published in French in 1972, the year I was born, and immediately translated into several languages.

[1] Case 106/77, *Simmenthal*, EU:C:1978:49; Case 22/70, *Commission v. Council* ('*ERTA*'), EU:C:1971:32; Opinion 1/78, EU:C:1979:224. These are only three among many leading judgments which bear the mark of Pescatore's approach.

[2] 'La carence du législateur communautaire et le devoir du juge', in G. Lüke and others (eds.), *Rechtsvergleichung, Europarecht und Staatenintegration: Gedächtnisschrift für Leontin-Jean Constantinesco* (1983) 559.

More than 40 years have passed since its publication and the Union and its law have changed a lot, but *Le droit de l'intégration*[3] can still be read with much profit, particularly in the present situation. Indeed, time may have rendered refreshing the content of this little book about how, for a number of European nations, the legal and institutional structures of the European Communities aimed to overcome the anarchical nature of the traditional international system, bringing those nations together under strong and lasting institutional and normative structures, solid enough to resist 'the onslaught of crisis and the erosion of time'.[4] From a legal perspective, the book explains that the Communities are based on a comprehensive and autonomous legal order, independent from the legal systems of the Member States and also from international law, and endowed with sufficient resources to tackle new problems. And it also presents the European Court of Justice as a key actor within that system.

Community law had to be autonomous, but I don't think Pierre Pescatore cared much about whether it was international or constitutional, or whether the Communities were a federal, confederal, or supranational entity. The subtitle of his book presents them as 'a new phenomenon in international relations': something at once innovative and traditional. His thinking was always beyond taxonomy. It focused on the structure and the functioning of the system. His main concern was whether integration could effectively and permanently transform the nature of the Member States and their relationships, disciplining their behaviour regardless of their transient political and economic preferences, and binding them together in a new autonomous organization.

He did not have a strong national identity and had a clear European calling, always and exclusively serving the European

[3] P. Pescatore, *Le droit de l'intégration: Émergence d'un phénomène nouveau dans les relations internationales selon l'expérience des Communautés européennes* (1972) (reprinted by Bruylant (2005)).

[4] Pescatore states that the stable structures of the Communities were '*capables de résister à l'assaut des crises et à l'érosion du temps*' (Pescatore, *supra* note 3, 2005 reprint, at 10).

general interest. It seemed to me that his European identity was stronger than his identity as a citizen of Luxembourg. His example was telling me that to practice Union law properly, to be a genuine European jurist, one should transcend one's national identity, as a lawyer and as a person, and leave it behind before entering the house of the law of integration. One should never say 'in my country', 'in my legal system', 'in your system', etc. We should understand that we own our shared European law, that it belongs to us, instead of seeing it as an essentially foreign, landless, and soulless object hanging in the air or fallen 'from Brussels'.

We had a few disagreements, of course, and they made our exchanges all the more interesting. There were three points, in particular, where we took slightly different views.

First of all, large as it was, Pescatore's mobile seemed to contain only the European system, conceived as a self-sufficient machine. He seemed to pay less attention to the various ways in which that machine was symbiotic with the national systems, and how that symbiosis has increased with its more recent evolution, so much so that it is very difficult to trace the boundaries between both levels. What we have today, perhaps, is an ever larger and more complex mobile with only fuzzy dividing lines: a convoluted 'fusion' of national and supranational political and legal mechanisms.

A second dimension to which Pescatore did not seem to pay close attention had to do with the various ways in which the economic system and its underlying interests, a crucial part of the enlarged mobile, interact with the legal and institutional systems, in a complex reciprocal co-determination. I always thought that the analysis of the Union system should not ignore the long, complex, and not unproblematic story of the relationship between the law of integration and capitalism or economic liberalism, and the consequences of that interaction for the European project at large.

Thirdly, I could not totally share his faith in the potential of law as a tool to civilize the behaviour of European nations. His belief in the power of law made me think at one point, while re-reading the *Pure Theory of Law*,[5] that Kelsen's theory was very

[5] H. Kelsen, *Pure Theory of Law* (1967) (translated by M. Knight).

similar to what the Court had been trying to do in the 1960s and 1970s: to build a 'pure theory' of Community law in the hope that it might lead one day to a more perfect practice of that law—but which was fated to encounter, in its unfolding, the various 'impurities' of legal practice. I could recognize the advantages of that 'candid' approach for a jurist, but for some reason I always felt unable to have such blind faith in integration or in law as its central tool. Hence in some of our discussions I ended up taking the role of a legal realist, recalling that in practice things rarely went the way theory wished they would go, and concluding that this mattered a great deal, as a legal order cannot be sustainable if the gap between norms and facts becomes so wide that the law's grasp upon reality becomes an illusion.

After our lunchtime conversations I went back to the Court. Sometimes elated, sometimes less so, I would see the old *palais*, which was being dismantled to take out the asbestos it contained. Some years later its austere original structure was surrounded by the new, larger, and flashy building of today. I sometimes thought that those architectural changes were an apt symbol of the new age, that the Court of that period was, deliberately or not, dismantling part of the old foundational case law, including some elements of the Pescatorian case law, whose excessively integrationist nature might have seemed toxic to some in the Europe of the new millennium. I did not see that, in spite of a number of concessions, the rusty beams of the old building—its essential structures—were being preserved and sometimes even reinforced. In reality, the Court of 15 years ago was resisting and preserving as much as it could. It was attempting a sort of containment and restoration work, in a context in which the forces of erosion, the pull towards disintegration, were already visible and quite strong. And yet, in retrospect, that period was rather benevolent towards European law when one compares it with more recent times.

Pescatore died in 2010. Sometimes I recall our conversations, very vividly, as though they happened yesterday. In the middle of my work I often say to myself: 'What would Pescatore do? How would he tackle this problem?' I also try to guess what he would think about the Union of today. Perhaps he would quickly head back to his grave, deeply depressed about the present state of things, recalling the times in which he could write a book of 100 pages containing the essentials of a complete and solid system which made perfect sense. Today the Union has grown exponentially in the number of Member States included, fields covered by its law, and case law. Its legal and institutional building has become complex and almost baroque. In some parts, a tired mannerism can be seen. Disagreement rages, and the indispensable consensus among the Member States about the basic meaning and implications of the Union is shrinking. More than a coherent mechanism, Pescatore might have the impression that he is looking at a capricious collection of contradictions and paradoxes. He could see that the mobile still moves, somehow, but less as an integrated system than as a chain of stochastic reactions, with entangled wires and broken elements. But perhaps he would remain optimistic and keep his usual faith, considering this or that modest or ambitious move, and believing that after a while integration and its law would remain in place, one way or another, strengthened by the worst crisis they have ever experienced.

What's left of the law of integration? is a real question, asked at a particular moment in history, about what remains of the law that Pierre Pescatore and others built for reasons they understood so well that they never paused to explain them—the reasons we may since have forgotten. It is a question about the current significance, if any, of that inheritance, which, like most inheritances, may become embarrassing if we do not know what to do with it.

What's left of the law of integration? is also an attempt at recovery, recognition, and resistance. Recovery of the initial meaning of legal integration, not as a historical exercise but as an exploration of its lasting significance. Recognition of the problems that legal integration has today, problems which, while not identical, resemble those encountered by previous generations of European lawyers. And resistance against the relentless march towards disintegration.

2

LAW AFTER AUSCHWITZ

Those who work with and reflect on Union law and national law at present no longer have had direct experience of the savagery of the bloody World Wars, with invasions, war crimes and genocide, due to endemic conflicts between the most civilized among the European nations, that twice devastated our continent in the last century.[1] We have not seen and can hardly imagine that wasteland, with starvation, displacement, epidemics, fractured societies, failed economies, failed political and legal systems, and failed constitutions. We have not seen it but we should remember what we did not see. If we do not, we may miss the whole point of the political and legal experiment of European integration, launched in the aftermath of the Second World War, by people who had lived through those experiences and survived, precisely with the aim of overcoming these horrors.

We have the history books. We have the archives. We have the memorials, the museums, the diaries, the memoirs, the novels, the documentaries, the films, the grim TV programmes shown late at night, not to be seen by children. How could one forget? Indeed, we do remember the suffering and the unthinkable atrocities which are epitomized in this most ominous word: *Auschwitz*. We have so much information about the last war that the whole of Europe could be plunged into a state of collective depression about its past. We do remember indeed, but at the same time we seem to have become insensitive to the lasting force of that historical experience, and do not realize that the world we live in was built upon those ruins and mountains of corpses, and because of them. We believe that Europe has changed, that only other peoples and other countries, in an inconceivable state of collective madness, could do such things

[1] This chapter and chapter 3 are based on 'Another Look at Constitutional Pluralism in the European Union', 22(3) *European Law Journal* 356.

What's Left of the Law of Integration? Decay and Resistance in European Union Law. First Edition. Julio Baquero Cruz. Published 2018 by Oxford University Press.

in a distant and barbaric period, and that something like that could never happen in the tolerant and quiet Europe of today, with the tolerant and quiet Europeans of today. We are so different! They were so different! We are so civilized! They were so barbaric!

There is something deeply troubling about our tendency to detach ourselves from the Europeans of only three or four generations ago. We remember, yes, but only as one remembers a vague nightmare quickly receding into darkness, protecting ourselves from those memories by removing their meaning for our present experience. The fossilization of memory is one of the most worrying symptoms of our contemporary Europe.

And so, perhaps unconsciously, we also increasingly detach European integration and its law from the extreme conditions which made them possible. For many years we have been approaching the Union as an ahistorical, amoral and purely technical object, and some question not only the legitimacy and wisdom of this or that policy choice, as happens in any political organization, but also the authority and structure of its law and institutions, and even its very existence or whether, following a utilitarian balancing of interests, it would be convenient for this or that country to withdraw from it. The prevailing mood seems to confirm, in a sort of self-fulfilling prophecy, that integration was just an instrument for the reconstruction of the nation state in post-war Europe, and for the pursuance of purely national economic interests, as Alan Milward suggested.[2] From this point of view, integration would have always been at war with itself, its success inevitably bringing forth its doom. At present, with the nation states arguably reconstructed—at least the most powerful ones—and often having widely diverging concerns and preferences, many are tempted to see integration as little more than an embarrassing left-over, with no intrinsic value—something that, for various reasons and from various sides, would have to be rolled back, downsized, phased out, transformed into a looser organization, or dismantled altogether.

[2] See A. Milward, *The European Rescue of the Nation-State* (2000).

It is this mood that reflects our blindness to historical experience, our detachment from it, our inability to learn from it. After Auschwitz, many asked themselves not only philosophical questions such as whether poetry could still be written or whether and how one could go on living,[3] but also more practical questions such as whether the politics and law of sovereign nation states could still be trusted as effective shields against the destructive forces lurking beneath the thin patina of European civilization. The post-war generation knew very well that those forces, ignited by blind nationalism, strong identities and an even stronger hatred for the other, were always ready to unleash their murderous rage in certain circumstances. In that context, surrounded by ruins of many kinds, many felt that serious efforts were required to restructure the European continent and to try to avoid a third—possibly final—World War.

European integration was an important part, in retrospect perhaps the most significant and successful part, of the plan to rebuild Europe on more solid foundations. The Council of Europe, with the European Convention on Human Rights, and the North Atlantic Treaty Organization, were other important elements of that plan, and there were more—but none had the institutional and legal ambition of the European Communities. National constitutional law was also deeply reformed, introducing powerful constitutional courts and a more robust protection of fundamental rights, and framing it into a system of supranational checks and balances. All these developments were about civilization, an existential enterprise in which legal and institutional architecture tried to overcome the moral bankruptcy into which Europe had fallen.

There had, of course, been 'a European system' before integration. The European nations engaged in trade, concluded alliances, cooperated in various ways and were closely interdependent. That system was defined as a 'balance of powers' in which war worked as the ultimate regulatory device when diplomacy failed. With technological progress and the new techniques of warfare, in the twentieth century that 'balance'

[3] Th. W. Adorno, *Negative Dialectics* (1990) (translated by E. B. Ashton), at 362 and 363.

became increasingly dysfunctional and almost suicidal for both European civilization and the human species at large.

From a supranational perspective, the most pressing thing to do was to bind the European states in a more formal framework, avoiding the floating nature of their traditional relationships, which international law, with its insufficient formalization and institutionalization, could do little to change. The simple idea of integration was to establish, among a group of states including at least France and Germany, common, permanent, independent, and effective institutions endowed with real powers which would act through law, framing the relationships between those states, initially in one strategic sector of the economic sphere and later on for the economy at large and atomic energy. The plan was to bind them together and to foster common interests and supranational solidarity in such a way and to such an extent that 'any war between France and Germany [would become] *not merely unthinkable, but materially impossible*', as we read in the Schuman declaration of 9 May 1950, the foundational document of integration.[4]

Besides its ultimate aim of establishing a European federation, its references to 'bloody divisions', peace, civilization, and solidarity, and a number of policy ideas, the Schuman declaration also contained some hints about the legal and institutional form of the proposed integration. There are several references to the creation of a common High Authority, endowed with real powers, whose decisions would be 'binding' and subject to appropriate judicial remedies ('*voies de recours*').

These few notions presupposed the creation of a number of legal and institutional structures, which were to take shape in the founding Treaties of Paris (1951) and Rome (1957). It is very rewarding to read those Treaties today, trying to forget what one knows about later interpretations, amendments, and additions. Some parts look like a normal international agreement, undoubtedly, but a significant number of elements were

[4] Available at www.robert-schuman.eu/en/declaration-of-9-may-1950 (emphasis added). On the drafting of the declaration and its follow-up, see H. Rieben and others (eds.), *Un changement d'espérance: La Déclaration du 9 mai 1950, Jean Monnet — Robert Schuman* (2000).

unprecedented in international legal instruments and remain unique to this day. They seem to belong to a different kind of organization.

Among them I will mention the following: the creation of common institutions endowed with decision-making powers enabling them to adopt secondary law, in some cases by qualified majority; the distinction between primary law and secondary law, and the principle of hierarchy of norms that follows from it; the 'direct applicability' of Regulations; the establishment of the Court of Justice, equipped with a complete procedural system and entrusted with the task of ensuring that the law is correctly interpreted and applied (instead of creating an arbitration tribunal that would rule *ex æquo et bono*); the preliminary rulings procedure, connecting national judges and the common Court; the principle of sincere cooperation between the Member States and the institutions; the unlimited duration of the European Economic Community; the establishment of a rigid Treaty amendment procedure, preserving the original pact; the treaty-making power of the Communities, conceived as international legal persons in their own right, and the procedure for the *ex ante* judicial review of international agreements to be concluded by them; and the inclusion of clear substantive rules limiting the powers of the Member States and sometimes also of private parties, such as the provisions on non-discrimination on the basis of nationality, the provisions on free movement, the provisions on equal pay for men and women, the competition rules, or the rules on state aid.

These legal and institutional structures cannot be seen as second-order choices, purely instrumental to the policy programme of the Treaties of Paris and Rome (the common regulation of coal and steel, the customs union, the common market, the common agricultural policy, the common commercial policy, etc.). The 'Community method' was not a consequence of overriding national economic interests, of hard intergovernmental bargaining and of the need to establish credible commitments.[5] Those preferences and bargains could have been pursued in the traditional

[5] This is the view of A. Moravcsik, *The Choice for Europe: Social Purpose & State Power from Messina to Maastricht* (1998) (see, in particular, chap. 7).

way, without any need to establish this highly innovative institutional and legal framework, which goes far beyond merely creating 'credibility'. Although economic incentives and inter-state negotiations clearly existed from the start, the legal and institutional structures of integration were a deliberate first-order choice—as important as, if not more important than, the accompanying policy measures. Those structures were and remain connected to the essential aim of integration: to establish an autonomous common organization that would secure lasting peace by changing the nature of the European states and of their relationships.

The fact that the scope of the initial treaties was confined to the economy, and the failure of the attempts to establish a European defence and political community, should not lead us to underrate their significance. There is a widespread viewpoint according to which integration was, and remains for the most part, economic and not political in nature. This perceived shortcoming is identified as the source of a congenital deficiency of the process, which would have to be remedied through a decisive leap into the higher plane of 'political integration'. This view is questionable. The economic sphere cannot be detached from the political sphere. Indeed, economic activity is a very important part of human activity, and economic integration entails political integration insofar as the economy is concerned. In addition to that, over time the scope of Union law has been enlarged beyond the economy, covering many other policy fields. One may dislike the politics of integration or one might want them to be structured in a different way, but it cannot be denied that from the start integration was an eminently political—and moral—enterprise. That was the view of the main actors involved at the time. In the meeting held in Bonn between Konrad Adenauer and Jean Monnet on 23 May 1950, shortly after the Schuman declaration, Adenauer declared that he did not approach the proposal from a technical perspective but as a high moral endeavour.[6]

[6] French minutes: '*M. Adenauer déclare que lui-même n'est pas un technicien; il n'est pas non plus à 100% un politicien. Il envisage lui aussi cette entreprise sous son aspect le plus élevé, et comme une entreprise d'ordre moral.*' German minutes: '*Der*

The words of the Treaties of Paris and Rome had to be given effect by the actors and procedures established by those very Treaties, and they were interpreted and applied by the Commission, the Council and the Court of Justice, and also by national authorities, including national courts. It was from these normative sources that the Court of Justice, their authoritative interpreter, deduced the basic characteristics of the law of integration in *Van Gend en Loos* (1963) and *Costa v. ENEL* (1964).[7]

The possibility given to individuals of relying on those rules of Community law which comply with the conditions of direct effect, and the obligation for national courts to enforce those rules against the Member States, if need be by setting aside any conflicting rule of national law, are fundamental assets of the law of integration. However, the simplistic equation of those two judgments with the technical tags of 'direct effect' and 'primacy' ignores an essential part of their significance as a matter of legal culture. From a systemic perspective one can learn much more from them.

Direct effect and primacy flow from the basic idea, which is the starting point of the reasoning, that the law of integration constitutes *a new legal order*. That was and remains the most far-reaching statement of those judgments. The basic traits of any legal order are its autonomy and its closure. A legal order is supposed to have a life of its own and to define its own nature, effects, and boundaries. Holding that the law of the Communities constitutes a new legal order, the Court means that it should not be seen as an amorphous collection of norms, as an excrescence of the laws of the Member States, or as part of international law. The Treaties, with all the elements mentioned above, are seen as an articulated and self-sufficient system, autonomous from international and national law, and closely

Bundeskanzler erklärte, er sei kein Techniker. Er stehe auch völlig auf dem Standpunkt, daß der Schuman-Plan in erster Linie eine moralische Angelegenheit sei.' The word '*moralische*' seems to be struck through and replaced by the word '*politische*' (*Un changement d'espérance*, *supra* note 4, at 246 and 252).

[7] Case 26/62, *Van Gend en Loos*, EU:C:1963:1; Case 6/64 *Costa v. ENEL*, EU:C:1964:66.

interconnected with the legal orders of those states. A second systemic consequence is that the norms of that legal order will be interpreted in accordance with its own methods, with a marked predominance of structure and *telos* over the elusive multilingual text. Finally, the Court makes clear that the law of the Communities will itself define the terms of its interaction with national law in a uniform manner, in contrast with ordinary international agreements, whose reception depends on the decision taken by each contracting party as a matter of national law. Institutionally, this also implies that it is for the Court of Justice, and not for state courts, to settle such matters.

Direct effect and primacy are thus logically implicit in the very idea of a new legal order. In turn, those principles only acquire their full meaning as the structural foundation of that order. Without them it would be impossible to see the law of integration structured as a legal *order*, as its relation with national law would depend on the unilateral choice of each national system. That law would diffract into a series of blurred reflections in the laws of the Member States—instead of having a solid and autonomous existence.

One should not forget, however, that the possibility of direct effect and primacy only becomes decisive for the civilizing prospects of the founding Treaties once the Court adds that the European rights which national courts must protect 'arise not only where they are expressly granted by the Treaty, *but also by reason of obligations which the Treaty imposes in a clearly defined way upon individuals as well as upon the Member States and upon the institutions of the Community*'.[8] This further interpretative move *enhances* the meaning of direct effect, with crucial structural consequences. Deducing individual rights from the obligations imposed on other individuals, on the Member States and on the institutions, the Court of Justice is maximizing the chances for the autonomy and effectiveness of the law of integration, for a real change in the relations between Member States, and for subjecting the institutions themselves to a shared rule of law. Finding those rights not only in secondary law but also in some

[8] *Van Gend en Loos*, *ibid*, at 12 (emphasis added).

provisions of primary law, the Court tends to entrench that autonomy and to ensure the irreversibility of certain commitments and a measure of intrinsic dynamism, while tracing its own sphere of power above the political institutions.

The reader will note that I have written: 'maximizes the chances', 'tends to entrench', etc. Like all judicial decisions, these judgments should be seen as complex speech acts. They did not just say things: they were meant to do something. They did not only represent a pre-existing reality: they acted upon it. But they could not achieve those things simply by stating them, in a sort of magical performance. In those acts of communication, much more was required: that the other relevant legal actors, including national authorities and courts and the other institutions of the Communities, should follow suit and behave in accordance with those principles. In *Van Gend en Loos* and *Costa v. ENEL* the Court was not laying down, once and for all, a shared European rule of law. It was only developing, in the wake of the Schuman declaration and of the drafters of the Treaties, the normative tools that could allow the law of integration to become an autonomous reality.

The most significant consecutive jurisprudential elaborations of that law are logical consequences of those two judgments. Among them, the following should be highlighted: the rejection of the principle of reciprocity and the obligation to comply with the law of the Communities regardless of the behaviour of other Member States; the possibility of enforcing some provisions against other individuals and not just against the states or the institutions; the confirmation that that law prevails over all conflicting national provisions, including constitutional provisions; the protection of the division of powers determined by that law; the potential liability of the Member States for harm due to breaches of Community law; and the protection of fundamental rights as an inherent requirement of the system.[9]

[9] See Joined Cases 90/63 and 91/63, *Commission v. Luxembourg and Belgium*, EU:C:1964:80; Case 43/75, *Defrenne*, EU:C:1976:56; Case 106/77, *Simmenthal*, EU:C:1978:49; and Case 22/70, *Commission v. Council* ('*ERTA*'), EU:C:1971:32; Joined Cases C-6/90 and C-9/90, *Francovich*, EU:C:1991:428; and Case 11/70, *Internationale Handelsgesellschaft*, EU:C:1970:114.

There was, as in other legal orders, a productive interaction between those who drafted and adopted the common rules and the organs to which they had decided—in the same rules—to entrust their interpretation and application. Regarding that interplay in the earlier years of integration, there is a widespread tendency to exaggerate the role played by the Court of Justice, in a fictional narrative which seems to look for an 'original sin' in the jurisprudential *acquis*. The proponents of this view see the Court as having 'created' direct effect, supremacy and all the rest in a series of 'bold' or 'revolutionary' decisions,[10] amounting to a 'juridical *coup d'État*'.[11] According to this view, the Court would have 'transformed' the Communities into something which no-one had ever envisaged,[12] betraying the 'real intentions' of the Member States.

From a similar perspective, in a late addition to Alan Milward's conception of integration as purely instrumental to the reassertion of the nation state in post-war Europe, the most recent historiography on Community law also sees the seminal judgments of the 1960s as a 'legal revolution' due to 'somewhat unorthodox', 'radical', or 'highly selective' interpretations of the Treaties.[13] In this view, the legitimacy of those judgments would be further weakened because they were the consequence of 'intense lobbying' by 'a small elite' organized in 'transnational networks of jurists sharing a common federalist ideology'.[14]

Many of these accounts ignore the basics of legal hermeneutics, and that renders them misguided. The Treaty of Rome had not stated anywhere that Community law could not have direct effect or that it could never prevail in case of conflict with

[10] See, e.g., Alter, 'Who are the "Masters of the Treaty"? European Governments and the European Court of Justice?', *International Organization* (2000) 489.

[11] Stone Sweet, 'The Juridical *Coup d'État* and the Problem of Authority: *CILFIT* and *Foto-Frost*', in M. Poiares Maduro and L. Azoulai (eds.), *The Past and Future of EU Law* (2010) 201.

[12] The language of 'transformation' was used by Weiler, 'The Transformation of Europe', *Yale Law Journal* (1991) 2403.

[13] Rasmussen, 'From *Costa v. ENEL* to the Treaties of Rome: A Brief History of a Legal Revolution', in Poiares Maduro and Azoulai (eds.), *The Past and Future of EU Law* (2010) 69, at 69, 74 and 75.

[14] *Ibid.*, at 78, 79 and 84.

national law. These points were left open and became a legitimate matter for judicial interpretation in the light of the text, structure, and purpose of the Treaty. In that regard, besides other important elements such as the direct applicability of Regulations, expressly recognized by that Treaty, or the creation of common institutions endowed with decision-making powers, the existence of the preliminary rulings procedure provided the decisive structural argument for direct effect.[15] On any reasonable interpretation, that procedure presupposed that Community law could be relevant in national judicial proceedings, and that private parties could invoke it before national courts. The principle of direct effect was, therefore, a fair deduction from the existence of the preliminary rulings procedure. By contrast, its rejection would have rendered nugatory the provision on that procedure. That interpretation would have been at odds with the legal materials.

The preliminary rulings procedure and direct effect inevitably raised the question of what to do in case of conflict between Community law and national law. Once again, that procedure contained a strong indication in favour of the primacy of Community law, as it provided that national courts of last resort were *bound* to refer preliminary questions if the provisions of that law were decisive for the case in hand. A reasonable interpreter would deduce from this obligation that the procedure was meant to ensure a uniform and effective application of Community law. And that should normally mean that the Court of Justice had the last word about its meaning and consequences. Again, it is the interpretation denying primacy to Community law that would have been a 'highly selective' reading of the legal materials.

As a matter of legal interpretation, therefore, the principles of direct effect, primacy and what follows from them fit much better with the normative content, structure and aim of the Treaties

[15] See *Van Gend en Loos*, *supra* note 7, at 12 of the judgment: 'In addition the task assigned to the Court of Justice under Article 177, the object of which is to secure uniform interpretation of the Treaty by national courts and tribunals, confirms that the states have acknowledged that Community law has an authority which can be invoked by their nationals before those courts and tribunals.'

than the opposite view. That view essentially requires one to believe that, despite the historical experience which brought the Treaties into existence, the declared political intentions behind them, and their striking differences from classical international agreements, the founders' answer to the events of the first half of the twentieth century was simply 'more of the same'.

As for the actors behind the attempt to establish a European rule of law, it should be quite clear that it was not a unilateral action by the Court of Justice. That objective can be traced to the authors of the Treaties, i.e. to the joint political decision of the six founding states, adopted and ratified by their competent institutions. In that context, the concrete positions adopted by the lawyers of the ministries of foreign affairs of some Member States in *Van Gend en Loos* cannot be equated with 'the position' of those states. The successive amendments to the Treaties never questioned direct effect and primacy, an essential part of the *acquis* that also had to be accepted by the Member States which joined later. The Court, on which the founding states had conferred jurisdiction to rule on those and other issues, only filled some gaps and clarified a number of open questions as soon as they were raised before it—connecting the dots, as it were, in the incomplete picture of which the Treaties were already the sketch. Although the early leading cases are indeed milestones in the story of integration, there is no 'original sin', no real 'constitutionalization', no 'transformation' of one thing into another, no 'break' or 'revolution', but rather the unfolding of a process that the Member States had themselves decided to set in motion, a process which they could no longer control unilaterally—*because that is what they had decided*—and which could naturally develop in that direction.

Having considered the reasons behind these developments, it is curious to see political scientists and even historians writing that this 'radical legal revolution' was carried out by a small transnational elite of jurists, pursuing marginal federalist ideas. That position, however, ignores the most obvious explanation. The word 'war' is hardly ever mentioned by those authors, as if it had disappeared from sight, and from such a state of amnesia it is indeed difficult to grasp the story of the law of integration. If one puts the war back into the picture, however, everything makes sense again, and there is no room for disingenuous conspiracy theories.

The most obvious explanation is, indeed, that it was as a reaction to the war, in the context of post-war reconstruction, that the original Treaties, as interpreted by the case law of the 1960s, set out to ensure that the Community became autonomous—more than the mere sum of its parts, a new political entity endowed with a life and a law of its own, which could not be determined unilaterally by any Member State, could deploy its effects following its own logic, and would effectively bind the states together within a common framework. From a historical perspective, that choice was the logical continuation of the movement started with the Schuman declaration. The opposite, i.e. the understanding of the law of integration as a mere excrescence of the laws of the Member States whose nature and effects would be unilaterally determined by the latter, would have been a crude betrayal of the idea of integration and a fatal blow to its civilizing potential.

Even though *Van Gend en Loos* and *Costa v. ENEL* do not mention it, the war could not have been far from the minds of the judges who decided those cases, in the same way as it could not have been absent from the minds of the drafters of the Schuman declaration or of the negotiators of the founding Treaties. For them, the legal and institutional structure of integration—the idea of a supranational legal order, direct effect, and supremacy—were not purely technical issues. They were moral and existential issues, matters of life or death, connected to the trenches, to aerial bombing and towns razed to the ground, to displaced populations, to concentration camps, to indelible wounds, and to family members lost in war. Beyond any more or less subtle legal argument from text, structure, or *telos*, it was the experience of war that gave them their mobilizing force. So much so that I sometimes think that the most fundamental reason justifying those Treaties and judgments remained mostly unspoken—except for the Schuman declaration.

How can that silence be explained? Perhaps it was so obvious at the time that there was no need to talk about it. Or perhaps the judges, prisoners of the formal rationality of law, could not allow themselves to refer to it. Or perhaps the trauma of war and the existential need to look ahead and not behind made it truly unthinkable and unspeakable. Perhaps the horror of the war was always unrepresentable, even for the law. But that silence in the early 1960s is full of meaning and should still speak to us with its original force.

The experience of war and barbarism at the heart of Europe was the fundamental explanation for the existence of the law of integration. Without it, integration and its law could never have come into existence and would not exist today. The Treaties should thus be seen not only as documents of civilization, but also as documents of the barbarism which made them possible.[16] I would say more. I would say that that experience should remain the main explanation for integration today. The possibility of war and, more generally, of radical conflict among the European nations should be the basis for the value we must give to the law of integration once we set out to assess its general state of health. From this perspective, the integrity of Union law should weigh rather heavily in the scales. If we give it less weight, if we are ready to sacrifice it, occasionally or permanently, for something else, we should explain the reasons for this sacrifice and be ready to accept its consequences.

This claim may seem odd to some, even to many. How could the war, a thing of a very distant past that we seem to have completely overcome, still be relevant for the contemporary practice of Union law? One of the first things I heard about integration, in a conference held in El Escorial in the summer of 1993,[17] was that the ideal of peace no longer had sufficient mobilizing force for the Europe of Maastricht. That ideal had been achieved long ago and we needed to look for a replacement to justify integration. Indeed, the Union spent the following decades searching for those new ideals. Various candidates included economic prosperity, the enlargement and 'reunification' of Europe after the cold war came to an end, the avoidance

[16] See Benjamin, 'Theses on the Philosophy of History', in *Illuminations*, translated by H. Zohn and edited by H. Arendt (1968) 252.

[17] This was a talk by Joseph Weiler which later became 'Fin-de-siècle Europe: Do the New Clothes Have an Emperor', in *The Constitution of Europe* (1999) 238.

of an environmental disaster, or the fight against international terrorism. Nevertheless, these alternatives offer a much less compelling rationale for integration and could at most be complementary to it. The strict framing of national sovereignty through common legal and institutional structures can hardly be justified by reference to the policy preferences prevailing among the states in this or that area, at this or that time. Even today, integration can only be properly understood as a conscious self-limitation and safeguard against the recurrent tragedies and lawlessness of war, i.e. as a means to secure peace.

We should thus never lose sight of war as the condition that made and makes integration possible. Even though war seems to have become 'materially impossible' among the states of the Union, we should be more lucid about human nature and nationalism and understand that war should always remain 'conceivable', even among the most civilized nations, as a distinct possibility. Otherwise we may become incapable of 'conceiving' integration. *If* we still can, that is.

Of course, 'war' is not only military: there is economic war, sometimes but not always leading to military war. There are cultural wars, institutional wars, cold wars, social wars, and even legal wars. There are also many more or less radical conflicts and disagreements which may deteriorate if they are not solved through mechanisms that are effective, and recognized as common, legitimate, and respected by all concerned—even if they do not always produce the result one would prefer. Could anyone be absolutely certain that—should the Union disintegrate, or be downgraded into a free trade area or a purely economic association, and the states regain full autonomy—there will be no more wars in Europe, in a more or less distant future?

From this perspective, the Member States and their peoples, some more than others but all of them, have a shared responsibility for Europe which springs from the common historical experience that binds them together. Without a sense of common responsibility, of overlapping consensus and identity, and without that historical consciousness, the Union would not be able to survive for long as a genuine system of integration. It could only be maintained as a voluntary and flexible association for the pursuance of a number of common interests, as long as they remain common, in a more classical international law framework in which the solidarity between the various states would be reduced to the bare minimum or excluded altogether. In that kind of association the basic aim of integration, now invisible as a result of our historical amnesia and—paradoxically—of its relative success, would quickly vanish.

This is not political science fiction. Powerful forces of various kinds are already at work in the Union system, pushing for its erosion and trying to transform it into that kind of looser association. Other forces tend to preserve the *acquis*, but their capacity to resist is not unlimited. In the meantime, the tension between these incompatible conceptions of what the Union is and what being a Member State entails, aggravated by a protracted crisis, has already had consequences for the common system, which shows various signs of strain and fragmentation, and maybe also of an incipient 'mutation'.[18] The negotiations undertaken by the then UK Prime Minister David Cameron in 2016, the ensuing stillborn deal, and the British referendum on withdrawal from the Union should be seen as the most remarkable, but by no means exclusive, symptom of this phenomenon.

If the Member States were not already bound by the existing system and structures of integration, which are protected by a rigid Treaty revision procedure, and were free to negotiate a new common framework, it is unclear whether a new agreement would be reached at all today. If it were reached, it would probably look very different from the Treaties we have inherited. This explains the current pressures for change and the contemporary malaise in integration. But the present mood is not only due to the various crises the Union is going through, the discontents and suffering they provoke, or the problems of design and legitimacy they reveal in a system which needs some serious fixing. It also tells us a lot about our loss of memory and understanding, which creates the risk of undoing integration instead of mending it, or of presenting its gradual undoing as a

[18] See Menéndez, 'A European Union in Constitutional Mutation?', 20(2) *European Law Journal* (2014) 127; but see, sceptical, Bruno De Witte, 'Euro Crisis Responses and the EU Legal Order: Increased Institutional Variation or Constitutional Mutation?', 11(3) *European Constitutional Law Review* (2015) 434.

mending of sorts, with the attendant risk of unleashing the forces which integration has helped to tame.

The rigidity of the Treaty amendment procedure, which became more rigid with every enlargement while the rule itself was never changed significantly, represents the weight of the past bearing down upon the present. It forces us to remember *procedurally*, even if we have forgotten. The weight of the past is felt in any event, though mostly as an oppressive force. That procedure preserves the *acquis*, but at the same time it makes optimal Treaty revisions very unlikely, entrenching major problems of constitutional design and leading to a continuous search for alternative ways of adapting the Union to difficult new circumstances. The rigidity of the revision procedure is a double-edged sword, protecting past integration while undermining it, and putting it at a great risk of implosion.[19]

[19] These questions will be explored in the penultimate chapter of this book (chapter 7).

3

AGAINST CONSTITUTIONAL PLURALISM

1

If integration can be seen as a complex process in which institutions, powers, interests, norms, principles, and values are in constant interaction, an essential element on which to test its state of health is the principle of primacy, the partial resistance to it by some national constitutional actors, and the sophisticated attempt to transcend this tension through the theory of 'constitutional pluralism'.[1] Together with direct effect, primacy embodies the force of Union law with regard to state law, redefining legal boundaries in Europe. Indeed, what is at stake in primacy is the very existence of the law of integration as an autonomous system—an existence that cannot be without consequences for the constitutional orders of the Member States. It is, therefore, a key issue as much for the Union as for its Member States.

Within its wide but limited scope of application, all Union law is held to prevail over all national law, including constitutional law, when a normative conflict arises. According to the case law of the Court of Justice, there are no limits to primacy, which is often characterized as an 'absolute' principle. The constitutional systems of the Member States generally accept the primacy of Union law, while asserting potential limits to protect their fundamental elements. In general those limits

[1] For my previous work on the subject, see 'The Legacy of the Maastricht-Urteil and the Pluralist Movement', 14(4) *European Law Journal* (2008) 389; 'An Area of Darkness: Three Conceptions of the Relationship between European Union Law and State Constitutional Law', in N. Walker and others (eds.), *Europe's Constitutional Mosaic* (2011) 49; and 'Legal Pluralism and Institutional Disobedience in the European Union', in M. Avbelj and J. Komárek (eds.), *Constitutional Pluralism in the European Union and Beyond* (2012) 249.

What's Left of the Law of Integration? Decay and Resistance in European Union Law. First Edition. Julio Baquero Cruz. Published 2018 by Oxford University Press.

remain hypothetical, and with very few exceptions there is a peaceful interaction between both positions. The fact remains, however, that their theoretical foundations are irreconcilable and that the absence of a common ground for a shared constitutional practice in the Union is a serious threat for the law of integration. In this context, constitutional pluralism claims to overcome the partial views of Union law and national constitutional law, proposing a new conception of supranational legal realities.

Resisting the allure of pluralism, this chapter argues that the approach of Union law to its relationship with national law is *preferable* to the other approaches. I use the word 'preferable' because, even if one were to accept that there is no undisputable basis for considering that this or that position is 'right' and this or that other one 'wrong', that this one is 'lawful' and that one 'unlawful', the fact remains that we should still discuss the various options in the light of their likely consequences, as a matter of practical reason.

2

In the first decades of integration, with the memory of war still vivid in the minds of national legal actors, there was a benevolent attitude towards the idea of a common legal order, at least *as a matter of theory*. Focusing on the paradigmatic German case, it is refreshing to read today an order of the German Constitutional Court of 18 October 1967.[2] In that decision, the German Court unanimously rejected as inadmissible a number of individual complaints, based on fundamental rights arguments, against acts of Community law. Its reasoning, closely following the jurisprudence of the European Court of Justice, recognized that the 'EEC Treaty is in a sense the constitution of [the] Community'. In turn, the Community was described as a 'new public authority . . . which is autonomous and independent vis-à-vis the public authorities of each Member

[2] Reproduced in A. Oppenheimer (ed.), *The Relationship between European Community Law and National Law: The Cases*, Volume 1 (1994) 410.

State', and whose acts 'do not require approval ("ratification") by the Member States nor can they be annulled by those States'.[3] A truly amicable and deferential approach is still visible in the *Kloppenburg* judgment of 1987,[4] in which the German Court stated that the European Court of Justice had 'the power of final decision on the interpretation of the Treaty and on the validity and interpretation of the acts of secondary Community law'—while voicing timid reservations. As will be explained in chapter 6, the *Solange I* judgment of 29 May 1974, on the protection of fundamental rights as regards Community law, reads as a provisional and moderate conditional reservation, especially when compared with more recent pronouncements; and in any event it was lifted by the *Solange II* judgment of 22 October 1986.[5]

One should not overlook, however, that the acceptance of the law of integration by national judiciaries always remained fragile *as a matter of practice*. Quite often one single national judgment was cited as authority for the proposition that primacy had been accepted—just as today many hasten to applaud a reference from this or that constitutional court, as though it marked a permanent structural shift. A single reference is, however, not enough to conclude that a general habit of compliance is in place and that the Union legal order is working as it is supposed to work.[6]

To be able to state that a legal system exists and functions smoothly, it is not enough to have rules, rights and obligations, procedures, and institutions. The actors concerned by them, from individuals to companies, from lawyers to public officials to judges and other competent bodies, should generally comply with those rules. If they are breached, there should be sufficient

[3] *Ibid.*, at 413. In the last part of the order the German Court reserved the question of whether it could review Community law with regard to fundamental rights, and to what extent, in other types of proceedings.

[4] *Ibid.*, at 497–519.

[5] *Ibid.*, at 440–60 (*Solange I*) and 462–96 (*Solange II*).

[6] The notion of a 'general habit of obedience' or compliance as a necessary element of a functioning legal order is due to J. Austin, *The Province of Jurisprudence Determined* (1995) (see, in particular, lecture VI).

remedies to obtain compliance or sanction non-compliance, so that the normative order does not become a castle of words hanging in the air. That general habit of compliance and the availability and effective use of those remedies constitute the criteria to assess whether the law of integration has reached maturity and achieved its aim, framing the deeply ingrained legal cultures of the Member States in an effective normative and institutional framework, i.e. in an overarching European legal culture.

From that perspective, one cannot ignore that in the real world the national legal systems and actors behaved—and often continue to behave—in ways which were (and remain) not strictly in line with the requirements of the law of integration. That law was not—and is not—always applied correctly by national authorities and courts. In particular, the obligation for national courts of last resort to refer issues of Union law to the European Court of Justice for a preliminary ruling has never been followed strictly, with negative consequences for the effectiveness and uniformity of that law. This means that the authority of Union law has always been much more fragile than one might deduce from the standard handbook on Union law. Across the Member States, political actors, national administrators, and judges do not always play the role assigned to them by the common system to its full extent. In most cases that partial neglect of Union law is not due to rebelliousness or to a wish to defend the national constitution, but to habit, expediency, ignorance, or sheer indifference. Quite often those actors do not feel that they are part of a wider system. They do not realize that Union law belongs to them and binds them for important reasons. Many of them still see Union law from a predominantly external perspective—as a foreign object, if they see it at all.

These are above all problems of legal culture and of the imperfect 'internalization' of the common system of law, problems that probably suffered a setback with each successive enlargement, since each time new legal cultures were added, with their own habits and entrenched attitudes. The formalization and discipline required by the law of integration, therefore, depends to a large extent on national political, administrative, and judicial processes which are not always predictable. Depending on the Member State, the actual *visible* incidence of Union law ranges from the anecdotal to the genuinely significant, but it cannot be said that it widely commands the sort of general habit of compliance found in mature and well-established legal orders. Its *invisible* impact, very often through national law transposing directives (the preferred instrument of secondary law), which then become indistinguishable from the mass of national law, can hardly be underestimated, but it is coupled with a measure of renationalization and fragmentation of Union law, as this is often applied in a purely national context, not following the Union law's own ways and logic.

These deficiencies were understandable in the first period of integration, in view of the persistence of national legal cultures and mentalities, and of the very novelty of the process. One might have hoped, however, that many decades later there would be more signs of a gradual coming together of the various elements, national and supranational, and of the consolidation of the shared legal culture without which the law of integration cannot function properly.

Paradoxically, the process seems to have been the opposite. In the early 1990s, the experience of the war and the perception of the need to bind the states into a formal system were fading away. At that time, many constitutional jurists of more recent generations, trained in a classical and dogmatic understanding of the nation state and its legal order, discovered the law of integration and found themselves in the middle of a nightmare in which they were losing their autonomy and also their *identity*. Indeed, identity, including legal identity, is a direct function of 'the other'. It needs to believe in the virtues of 'our system' or 'our legal tradition', as opposed to other traditions. It cannot maintain its claim to solidity without the 'other'.

When the national constitutional lawyer awoke from that nightmare, he tried to analyse it and to make it fit into his domestic reality. This is the origin, reflected in a series of judicial decisions (mainly in Germany and Italy), of the mainstream position of national constitutionalism vis-à-vis legal integration. This position found its most articulated expression in the Maastricht judgment of the German Constitutional Court, of

12 October 1993,[7] and it later spread to many Member States,[8] although not all of them, with some variations.

In that new position, the constructive and deferential discourse of the past was reduced to a side gesture of 'cooperation', 'responsibility', or 'openness' towards integration, while the previous timid provisional reservations became the central discourse, crystallizing in a conception in which Union law is exclusively seen through the lens of national constitutional law. From that perspective, the authority of Union law could not be founded on the Treaties themselves, which are not the creation of an original constituent power, but on the clauses within the national constitutions which allow for the transfer of the exercise of certain powers to the institutions of the Union. The primacy of Union law would thus only be recognized if and insofar as the applicable national constitution authorizes it, and would be subject to a number of limits aimed at preserving the core values and principles of that constitution. Those limits usually relate to the protection of fundamental rights, the boundaries of Union competences and the *identity* of those constitutions. This discourse is based on the sovereign power of the constitutional subject—an original, indivisible, and mythical power which could never be affected by the non-original, partial, and secular power which produced the law of integration. Often, it also refers to the protection of the allegedly more democratic processes established by national constitutions.

Nevertheless, as though seized by an attack of constitutional vertigo, the relevant national actors always stopped short of all the logical consequences to which their approach would seem to lead. National constitutional courts were prudent and, perhaps keeping a remnant of historical memory regarding the basic aim of integration, avoided clashes that could fatally undermine the shared system of law. Indeed, it might have been expected

[7] BVerfGE 89, 155 (1993). English translation in (1994) 69(2) *Common Market Law Reports* 57.

[8] In a recent decision, the German Constitutional Court refers to the constitutional case law of 10 Member States, where a comparable approach to the relationship between Union law and state constitutional law has been followed (order of 14 January 2014, DE:BVerfG:2014:rs20140114:2bvr272813, at para. 30).

that the imperative of protecting the will of an original constituent power, supposedly absent in the Union, should have led to a vigorous defence of the constitution as a whole. By contrast, the mainstream national position accepts the primacy of Union law over the national constitution, except for a core of fundamental rules and principles. And, even then, it would only be in the rare hypothetical case of a structural or manifest breach of that core that a constitutional court would consider asserting its power to limit the primacy of Union law. This limited defence of the state constitutional order shows that the relevant national actors implicitly acknowledge or at least tolerate most of the overriding legal force of the founding pact of integration. That attitude is reasonable, because a distinction between the 'original' constituent power of the states and the composite 'non-original' power behind the Union, taken to the extreme, would create conditions where it would be very difficult for Union law to operate properly.

It might also have been expected that the protection of national democratic processes, a theme that is shared by some strands of the pluralist movement and to which I will return later, should have led to a robust defence of *all legislation* adopted by the allegedly more democratic national legislature. Instead, the primacy of Union law over national legislation is generally accepted, and the potential limits only concern the core of state constitutional law. It is hard to see how this would protect the outcomes of national democratic processes. This attitude shows that national actors implicitly accept that the decision-making process of the Union, whatever its defects, is sufficiently democratic to command legal respect.

In spite of a generally prudent practice, the theoretical reconstruction of the relationship between the law of integration and state law due to the approach taken by some national legal actors remained in place and became widespread among the Member States. While for many years it did not have major consequences, besides the indirect pressure put on the European Court of Justice and on the other Union institutions, in the present context of crisis it appears as if constitutional vertigo is sometimes defied and even courted. Let me give some examples.

In one case, a rather unfortunate constitutional *imbroglio* tinged with national pride, the Czech Constitutional Court declared *ultra vires* a rather straightforward judgment of the European Court of Justice which had recognized the right of Slovak nationals to receive a supplementary pension payment on the same terms as Czech nationals.[9] The Czech Constitutional Court approached Union law as international law, ignoring its specificity. While failing to send a preliminary reference, it curiously complained that the Court of Justice had not heard its views before issuing its preliminary ruling—which was prompted by a prior reference from the Supreme Administrative Court of the Czech Republic—considering that the 'fairness of the trial' was affected.

In a second case, the German Constitutional Court referred to the European Court of Justice an issue of Union law of vital importance for the future of integration: whether the outright monetary transactions (OMT) programme of the European Central Bank, which aimed to ensure monetary stability in the euro area as a whole, was compatible with Union law. In doing so, however, it exerted significant pressure on the Court of Justice, threatening non-compliance if the Court did not follow its preferred interpretation. Thus, the referring court held that '[s]ubject to the interpretation by the Court of Justice of the European Union, the Federal Constitutional Court considers the OMT Decision [of the European Central Bank] incompatible' with various provisions of Union law, and announced that it would declare it unconstitutional unless the Court of Justice interpreted that Decision in line with the detailed conditions set out in the preliminary reference,[10] conditions which could seriously hamper its effectiveness.

In its judgment, the Court of Justice confirmed the validity of the European Central Bank's decision, recalling the conditions laid down in it but disregarding the additional requirements of

[9] See the judgment of the Czech Constitutional Court of 31 January 2012, CZ:US:2012:Pl.US:5:12:1; Case C-399/09, *Landtová*, EU:C:2011:415.

[10] Order of the Second Senate of the German Constitutional Court of 14 January 2014, DE:BVerfG:2014:rs20140114.2bvr272813, at paras. 55 and 100.

the German Constitutional Court.[11] One might have thought that that would have settled the legal issue, as the court with jurisdiction to rule on the legality of Union measures had declared the Bank's decision lawful. Nevertheless, it took the German Court a year and a new hearing before it rejected the applications against the OMT decision. And it did so after a 'creative' reading of the judgment of the Court of Justice, which was partly bent to make it fit within the Procrustean bed of the preliminary reference.[12]

Even though a serious constitutional, economic, and political conflict was averted, from a structural perspective this case is a worrying symptom of a decaying legal landscape. In more than six decades of integration, we had never before seen a preliminary reference which openly questioned and tried to pre-empt the authority of the Court of Justice to interpret Union law and rule on its validity. Besides, this is not the end of the story. The judgment of the European Court was respected as to the result but its normative underpinnings were distorted, leaving a measure of uncertainty about the acceptance of the European Central Bank's powers and the policy tools it needs to ensure the sustainability of the common currency.[13] This is regrettable in itself and also in view of the example the German Court seems to set for the constitutional courts of other Member States.

In a third case, the Supreme Court of Denmark sent to the Court of Justice a preliminary reference asking whether the general principle of non-discrimination on grounds of age precluded Danish rules which, under some conditions, deprived an employee of certain rights depending on his or her age. The judgment of the Court of Justice was clear: Union law precludes

[11] Case C-62/14, *Gauweiler*, EU:C:2015:400.

[12] Judgment of 21 June 2016, DE:BVerfG:2016:rs20160621.2bvr272813. See Payandeh, 'The OMT Judgment of the German Federal Constitutional Court', *European Constitutional Law Review* (2017) 400.

[13] That the European Central Bank's authority remains contested is shown by a second preliminary reference from the German Constitutional Court on a similar issue, this time relating to the Bank's 'Expanded Asset Purchase Programme' (order of 18 July 2017, 2 BvR 859/15, DE:BVerfG:2017:rs20170718.2bvr085915, which has resulted in Case C-493/17, *Weiss and others*, currently pending before the Court of Justice).

such rules and the referring court was bound to interpret the Danish provisions in conformity with Union law, which seemed feasible in view of the wording of those provisions. In any event, if consistent interpretation were not possible, the Danish Court would have to set them aside.[14] After receiving the ruling, the Danish Court found that a consistent interpretation was impossible—although this was only in respect of its own case law, not in relation to the text of the law. Quite surprisingly, it went on to hold that the Danish act of accession did not empower it to give precedence to unwritten general principles of Union law over conflicting provisions of Danish law in the context of disputes between private parties, thus disregarding the judgment of the Court of Justice and the right granted by the general principle of Union law.[15]

This third episode is most perplexing, as a preliminary reference was requested, a clear answer was given by the Court, and the Danish Supreme Court, the last judicial instance of a Member State, openly disrespected it. It is also worrying in view of the key role that general principles of law have always played, through case law dating back to the 1950s,[16] in the law of integration, and of the impact this national case law could have for the future application of the Charter of Fundamental Rights in Denmark as regards disputes between private parties. While the Union system is not impotent when it encounters that kind of institutional defiance, as will be shown in the following chapter, the Danish case gives a strong impression of systemic failure, and nothing seems to have been done in response to it.

Finally, in a recent preliminary reference following the judgment in *Taricco*,[17] the Italian Constitutional Court questioned the interpretation of the principle of legality in criminal law contained in that judgment, in view of the stricter standard of

[14] Case C-441/14, *Dansk Industri*, EU:C:2016:278.

[15] Case 15/2014, *Ajos*, judgment of 6 December 2016 (English translation available at www.supremecourt.dk/supremecourt/nyheder/pressemeddelelser/Documents/Judgment%2015-2014.pdf).

[16] Joined Cases 7/56, 3/57 to 7/57, *Algera*, EU:C:1957:7.

[17] Case C-105/14, *Taricco*, EU:C:2015:555.

protection provided by the Italian Constitution. In *Taricco*, the Court of Justice held that Italian criminal courts had to set aside a particular aspect of the national rules on the interruption of limitation periods if it led to impunity in a significant number of cases of serious VAT fraud, rendering the protection of the Union's financial interests ineffective. While the legal orders of most Member States and the European Court of Human Rights consider rules on limitation periods as procedural provisions not covered by the principle of legality, allowing for the position taken by the Court of Justice, Italian constitutional and criminal law see those rules as substantive law protected by that principle, thus objecting to *Taricco* and requiring the full application of the rules that were in force at the time of the offence. The Italian Court suggested an overruling, or else the recognition of a specific position for Italy, based on Article 53 of the Charter or on Article 4(2) of the Treaty on European Union (TEU). Otherwise, it threatened to disregard *Taricco* in order to protect the Italian Constitution, which would lead to an ineffective protection of the Union's financial interests.

In its judgment of 5 December 2017, the Court of Justice implicitly overruled *Taricco* in part, avoiding a constitutional conflict and accepting, on a provisional basis, the potentially defective protection given by Italy to the financial interests of the Union. However, the grounds and bounds of this exception are not clearly articulated, and this leads to uncertainty about its temporal scope and, more generally, about the conditions under which a stricter national standard for the protection of fundamental rights may justify an exception to the normal application of Union law.[18]

If we put it in historical perspective, the evolution of the position of some national constitutional actors as regards Union law could be seen as a consequence of the perceived reconstruction of the nation state as a political organization: the more the Member States are felt to be 'reconstructed', the more ambivalent their stance on the law of integration. This vindication of the political and legal pre-eminence of the nation state probably

[18] Case C-42/17, *M.A.S. and M.B.*, EU:C:2017:936.

reached its apogee with the Lisbon judgment of the German Constitutional Court, which proclaimed that 'the State is neither a myth nor an end in itself but the *historically grown* and *globally recognised* form of organisation of a *viable political community*'.[19] In its historical amnesia, this assertion could give serious cause for concern, as integration is not recognized for what it is: the overarching political community that ensures the long-term viability of the nation state.

While these more recent examples show a shift and a measure of decay in the midst of the constitutional and economic crisis of the Union, they are the exception rather than the rule. For the most part, a mixture of correct engagement and substandard practice remains. The approaches of Union law and state law to their interaction are diametrically opposed in theory and seem to create conditions where it will be very difficult for the former to be fully effective. Nevertheless, the two legal orders seem to rub along quite comfortably in practice, leading quiet parallel lives. The European system does so through a relaxation of its discipline and through increasing accommodation,[20] so much so that sometimes the real danger is not direct conflict but rendering Union law so flexible that it may become irrelevant. And national constitutional systems accommodate integration by reducing their claims to the notional preservation of a small shrine of constitutional identity.

This is the pragmatic view: the underlying reasons do not matter as long as the results are compatible and we arrive at the same destination or meet somewhere along the way. According to this view, it is unimportant whether you arrive at the same results through the national constitution or through Union law, as long as a meeting takes place.

It cannot be denied that the *modus vivendi* based on appeasement and institutional diplomacy is better than nothing, but it is risky in view of the disagreement about its underlying grounds.

[19] Judgment of 30 June 2009 (DE:BVerfG:2009:es20090630:2bve000208), at para. 224 (emphasis added).

[20] On these strategies of accommodation, see Azoulai, 'The Future Constitutional Role of the European Court of Justice', in J. Baquero Cruz and C. Closa (eds.), *European Integration from Rome to Berlin: 1957–2007* (2009) 229.

In law, reasons are always much more important than outcomes. The persistent disagreement about the grounds and nature of the authority of Union law, and about the correct path of argument to take certain decisions, makes the compromise inherently ambiguous and fragile. At any point in time a constitutional actor in any Member State may consider that the compromise must be broken for this or that reason, and at that point it is probably Union law which will be disregarded. With such a large number of Member States, the risk of constitutional stupidities, accidents, and tragedies has become very high.

3

Constitutional pluralism was conceived in the troubled waters of the 1990s, more or less at the same time as some national constitutional doctrines set out to downplay the law of integration, considering it as a tolerated and limited phenomenon. In historical terms, pluralism belongs to an era characterized by a loss of memory, a disconnection between war and European integration, and an increasing reassertion of national constitutionalism. A historical understanding of the aim of integration is thus largely absent in the pluralist literature, which seems to be playing a sophisticated board game with abstract notions, devoid of any historical or practical background. In that context, faithful to the spirit of its times, constitutional pluralism also ends up justifying a weakening of the discipline of integration.

It could be thought that the 'pluralists' (i.e. Neil MacCormick,[21] their *maître à penser*, followed by Neil Walker, Mattias Kumm, and Miguel Maduro,[22] themselves followed by some

[21] MacCormick, 'Beyond the Sovereign State', 56(1) *Modern Law Review* (1993) 1; 'The Maastricht-Urteil: Sovereignty Now', *European Law Journal* (1995) 259; and *Questioning Sovereignty: Law, State and Nation in the European Commonwealth* (1999).

[22] See Walker, 'The Idea of Constitutional Pluralism', 65 *Modern Law Review* (2002) 317; Maduro, 'Contrapunctual Law: Europe's Constitutional Pluralism in Action', in N. Walker (ed.), *Sovereignty in Transition* (2003) 501; Kumm, 'The Jurisprudence of Constitutional Conflict: Constitutional Supremacy in Europe before and after the Constitutional Treaty', 11 *European Law Journal* (2005) 262.

younger scholars)[23] have such divergent views that they do not form a coherent movement. There are several pluralisms, so different that one kind would not accept the other as pluralist, leading to endless internal debates. In this doctrinal confusion, what does pluralism stand for, beyond the natural variations between different authors?

In substance, what all of them have in common is that they purport to reject the approaches taken by Union law and national law towards their reciprocal relations, seeing them both as 'monist' and incommensurable, claiming that each is valid within its own system and that there is no way to reconcile them in some external comprehensive view. Therefore, they reject 'hierarchy' as a contemptible word and hasten to embrace 'heterarchy',[24] favouring open-ended processes of informal dialogue and spontaneous mutual adjustment. In that 'heterarchical' space, they try to maintain a neutral position, without taking sides. In consequence, they would prefer to leave the issue of primacy permanently open and undecided, and admit unilateral exceptions based on the need to preserve the constitutional identity or the democratic processes of each Member State. Some pluralists try to frame those exceptions more or less strictly by identifying the cases in which a national constitutional court would have *the final say* over the Court of Justice (Kumm), or by elaborating a set of common interpretative principles aimed at reducing disagreement (Maduro and, to a certain extent, Walker).

If this is what constitutional pluralism stands for, it seems to me that it has serious problems as a description, for things are not always as it claims they are, and also as a prescription, because it does not offer an attractive and sustainable model for the

[23] Krisch, *Beyond Constitutionalism: The Pluralist Structure of Postnational Law* (2010); Jaklic, *Constitutional Pluralism in the EU* (2014); M. Avbelj and J. Komárek (eds.), *Constitutional Pluralism in the European Union and Beyond* (2012).

[24] The word exists, but the *Oxford English Dictionary* declares it 'obsolete'. In reality it does not mean 'rule by the many', but 'the rule of an alien'. In his famous dictionary, Samuel Johnson defined it as the 'government of an alien', giving as an example a quotation from Bishop Hall which embodies what constitutional pluralism leads to: 'next to anarchy is *heterarchy*' (Johnson, *A Dictionary of the English Language*, volume 2 (1818 edn.)).

relationship between the legal systems involved. Indeed, in prescriptive terms constitutional pluralism is a deeply disturbing doctrine regarding the way in which Union law and the laws of the states should interact, because it undermines the main objective of integration and the basic social function of law.

In their account of the legal landscape, the pluralists never pause to consider the significant practical problems encountered by Union law in commanding a general habit of compliance in the Member States. They do not seem to be interested in the everyday life of law, but only in extraordinary and exceptional cases of disagreement. Their analysis takes for granted that the normative claims of Union law are generally effective and that both systems routinely enter into radical contradictions, while the opposite is true: contradictions are rare, practice less than virtuous. The discourse of constitutional pluralism is built on the basis of this unrealistic assumption. I tend to think, in contrast, that the imperfect practice of Union law should be the starting point of any discussion about its relationship with state law.

Secondly, for all its worth as an element of liberal political organizations and processes, when it enters the realm of law pluralism acquires a very different meaning. And constitutional pluralism was and remains, for the most part, a legal doctrine. In law, pluralism enters into conflict with one of the main objectives of any legal system as a tool of civilization, which is to achieve order, security, predictability, and certainty in social and institutional relationships, in a person's position, rights, and obligations vis-à-vis other people and public authorities. That's one of the basic things—if not the main thing—that law and only law can bring. Predictability is closely connected to the general habit of compliance. If one does not know which rule applies or what is its correct meaning, how may one comply with it?

Physical and legal persons, public and private entities, should know where they stand and be able to regulate their behaviour beforehand, in contract law, family law, criminal law, economic regulation, etc. If the law is too uncertain, the legal system is not functioning correctly. Admittedly, there is always a degree of uncertainty in law, but legal and institutional systems aim to reduce this as much as possible. It is curious to see, from the 1990s onwards, European jurists proposing a legal practice that would render the meaning of law in Europe ever more uncertain.

The expression 'legal (or constitutional) pluralism' may thus be little more than an oxymoron.[25] In view of its social function, law tends to be an ordered system of norms and must pursue that order. Since constitutional pluralism is based on unstructured dialogues and accepts derogations to primacy (subject to hazy limits) as spontaneous and even welcome traces of 'heterarchy', thus leading to disorder, that theory cannot be trusted to organize the relationships between legal systems in an acceptable way.

If law is only plural because the society and political community in which it is produced is plural, then the term 'constitutional pluralism' does not have a distinct meaning—and indeed it is not in this sense that the expression is used by the pluralists. The law of a plural society with open institutions will necessarily reflect the characteristics of that society. It is not doubted that the Union should be plural in that sense. But it is another matter to claim that the judicial application of that law should be entrusted to an open and partly unpredictable web of poorly coordinated actors. That would lead to an unhealthy 'politicization' of law, with the temptation of selective and unilateral judicial disapplication or misapplication of Union law, and the corresponding decay of the European political process due to the multiplication of constitutional veto positions. This would be worrying because the distinction between the spheres of law and politics, and the ensuing specialization of work between them, is a precious asset in modern political communities. An asset on which European integration is also based.

This discussion is connected to the idea that constitutional pluralism, with its potential limits to the primacy of Union law, could protect the more democratic political processes of the Member States. That justification seems to me to be misconceived for various reasons.

[25] See, from a different perspective, Loughlin, 'Constitutional Pluralism: An Oxymoron?', *Global Constitutionalism* (2014), at 9–30.

The first one is that a robust rule of law is a crucial structural element of any democracy.[26] In the gradual construction of the modern polity, law always comes before democracy, historically and logically. There may be a functioning but more or less undemocratic 'rule of law', but there can be no genuine democracy without the rule of law. Democracy requires that the decisions taken by the representative organs of the polity, reflected in law, are effectively implemented and enforced, acting upon social reality. Without the rule of law, those organs would be impotent and democracy would be a purely formal exercise. This means that there can be no trade-off between the rule of law and democracy. Pretending to defend national democratic processes by selectively damaging the European rule of law is therefore inconsistent. That kind of behaviour simply undermines the rule of law without improving the democratic life of the Union or of its Member States.

Secondly, if the Union were a grossly undemocratic regime the correct thing for the Member States to do would be to try to democratize it or, if they did not manage this, to leave it or to dismantle it altogether. But the Union is not a grossly undemocratic or authoritarian regime. In fact, it is not even mildly undemocratic. Democracy is never pure—it is always imperfect and hybrid, never fully attaining the democratic ideal, always adjusted to particular circumstances, always changing and improvable. From that perspective, while the political structures of the Union do not correspond to those of centralized nation states and are adapted to its specific needs, the Union is not undemocratic. It is not an authoritarian or tyrannical regime whose law one might rightfully disobey.

The Union is organized as a sort of consociational democracy, with the advantages and disadvantages of that model. According to the theory of consociational democracy,[27] polities that are divided along rigid lines, such as linguistic, ethnic, or religious

[26] In this I would disagree with one of the main authorities on the subject, for whom the rule of law is 'helpful' but would not be among the 'crucial' preconditions of democracy (Dahl, *On Democracy* (1998), at 159).

[27] See, for an introduction, Lijphart, 'Constitutional Design for Divided Societies', 15(2) *Journal of Democracy* (2004) 96.

differences, and between which there are high levels of mistrust, sometimes still prefer to remain together because for various reasons they value being together more than being apart. In such systems, standard democratic arrangements are modified in a number of ways, most significantly by limiting simple majority rule, which would often be hard to accept, and favouring consensual decision-making through large coalitions. The drawbacks of such systems are their relative fragility, the limited role of opposition, their elite-driven character, the frequent need for a measure of secrecy in negotiations, and the risk of minority veto positions or paralysis. A democratic arrangement of this kind is clearly at work in the Union, which is divided along national lines, but that does not mean that the Union undermines the democracies of the Member States. It simply means that it has the sort of democracy that it can bear in view of its underlying political and social conditions. The deepening of the system towards more majoritarian forms of decision-making would entail a risk of instability, and could only be introduced gradually and carefully, once those conditions had evolved to a point where they would allow this.

Finally, in spite of its shortcomings, the consequences for the democratic life of the Member States of even this 'adapted' democracy are largely positive, because it enlarges the territorial scope of democratic decision-making and allows for decisions that affect all the states and their peoples to be taken in common. The alternative of allowing the Member States to take decisions that would have important effects outside their borders, affecting persons and interests which were not represented in those systems, is not more democratic, even if one conceded that national political processes are organized along more democratic lines. In addition, the particular political conditions of the Union, with the absence of an entrenched party system and of a lasting political majority, can lead to a democratic debate which is much more open and dynamic than that within the states, as specific support has to be gathered for every new legislative proposal.

If democratic concerns do not justify the pluralists' position, neither does their idea that the Union and the national constitutional positions are all *monist* and fully *symmetrical*, which is the basis for their proposal of a third allegedly 'superior' way between those extreme 'monist' positions. I have already explained that the existing positions are not extreme in practice. Besides, the Union position cannot be qualified as monist and is not the symmetrical counterpart of the national positions.

The position of Union law regarding its relationship with national law, as articulated by the Court of Justice, is clearly a dualist position, but one of ordered and not of chaotic dualism. Union law does not claim to trace back all law applicable in the territory of the Member States to a single integrated legal order, of which the national laws would just be 'delegated' appendices. Union law has never claimed that national law is derived from it or hierarchically inferior to it. Union law simply states that it is autonomous and has the authority to determine its own effects, regulating conflicts with national law in the way which best preserves its integrity as a shared partial system of law. Beyond that, Union law has little to say about the nature, validity, or authority of national law. The Union does not pretend to have its own sovereignty, only to frame national sovereignty in part. The law of integration has therefore been 'beyond sovereignty' from the start.

By contrast, the national constitutional position may strictly be referred to as a monist position—at least as a matter of theory. Indeed, a considerable number of constitutional courts in Europe consider that *all* the law applying in the territory of their state, including Union law, should be traced back to the national constitution. As explained above, national constitutional law claims to determine not only primacy and its limits, but also the effects that Union law has in the national legal system. Through this very artificial device, national constitutional law becomes the normative space where the laws of Europe are reordered into 28 monist units.

The absence of symmetry between the Union position and the national constitutional positions refutes the pluralists' claim about the need for an external common order that could regulate inter-systemic relationships. This rather disconcerting claim ignores the fact that Union law constitutes a system of law shared by the Member States and has an overarching character that the constitutional orders of the states could never have.

If any legal system in Europe is well-placed to regulate inter-systemic relationships in an ordered and effective way, that system is the common system, not the particular systems of the states—or a potential third system above all of them. Certainly, this approach takes the importance of maintaining ordered relationships for granted, but in view of the historical roots of integration and of the essential functions of law that objective cannot be seriously denied.

The point, which is a rather simple one, is that in the normative space covered by Union law each Member State is meant to be bound by the same rules and that each accepts the constraints of those rules because it can trust that the others will do the same. That state of legal affairs is in their mutual interest, as an essential element of the political stability and peace that integration ensures in Europe. By contrast, if one Member State can have unilaterally defined constitutional limits to primacy, then all the states will want them too. In this game, some positions will be much more powerful than others, leading to inequality and political domination. That proliferation of constitutionally protected veto positions would fatally damage the existence of a common rule of law, fragmenting the Union and leading back, at least in part, to the international law paradigm.

Among the pluralists, those who have more legal common sense perceive this risk and invariably end up trying to reconstruct an integrated system, be it through process and interpretative principles (Walker, Maduro), rediscovering the good old public international law whose shortcomings integration was supposed to overcome (MacCormick), or through balancing and accommodation (Kumm). In a curious development, their pluralism takes the problem to another normative sphere and tries to find a solution there. However, that putative sphere ends up resembling very much those we already know.

Thus, a pluralist scholar like Kumm often seems to be elaborating the theoretical underpinnings of the approach of the German Constitutional Court by defining the cases in which *the final word* (for in litigation there must always be a final word) would be for that or other constitutional courts and not for the European Court. On the other hand, authors like Walker or Maduro seem to be proposing a thinner version of the law of integration (this time supposedly no longer negotiable) which would be superimposed on both the Union and the national systems. That thinner version would hold the two levels together without degenerating into a 'monist' order. However, since that meta-framework has to be shared by all if it is to work, it will probably become 'monist' in turn and thus give rise to further conflicts, requiring an ever thinner meta-meta-framework placed at a different and more abstract level. And so on and so forth, in a potentially infinite regression, until we reach the point in which the idea of a law common to all, and integration itself, vanish in the air, i.e. until we are left with the solid stone of national constitutional law. Taken to its extreme derivative, this is where constitutional pluralism seems to lead.

At bottom, the various pluralist strategies to clean up the mess of 'heterarchy' look like variations of the national constitutional position. And it is hard to see what a virtuous practice of pluralism would look like, especially if one takes into account the recent constitutional accidents mentioned above. A difficult decision may be deferred for a while, but it cannot be postponed forever. In the same way, the issue of primacy may be left open in general (with negative consequences for the integrity of Union law), but it cannot be left open in each particular case. After deciding it in a series of cases, a sort of rule will have been established. At some point neutrality cannot be maintained and a decision must be taken if the legal order is to produce meaning. At that point, since they do not want to defend the classical approach of Union law, the pluralists accept a number of potential exceptions to the primacy of Union law and to the 'final word' of the European Court of Justice, thus damaging the integrity of the common legal system. This is just what some national constitutional courts do.

When pressed in theory or in practice, therefore, constitutional pluralism tends to dissolve into an ever thinner version of Union law or into an expression of national constitutional thinking, compromising the basic aim of the law of integration. For this meagre and dubious result, one wonders whether the arduous theoretical journey of the pluralists was really worth the effort.

These practical and theoretical blind alleys show that the resistance to the primacy of Union law embodied in constitutional pluralism is not really or mainly either about preserving a 'heterarchical' space between the Union and the states, about improving Union law and its relationship with national law, or about reinforcing democracy. In reality it is about power and it is also linked, perhaps unconsciously, to the reassertion of the nation state as an organizational entity. In this, constitutional pluralism may also be seen as a symptom of the contemporary anxiety about identity and of the loss of memory regarding the crucial stakes of European integration. To that extent, there can be no doubt that it is *politically correct*—also in a literal sense, i.e. fitting with widespread contemporary political conceptions, however misconceived they may be.

This political dimension also means that constitutional pluralism, like the national constitutional positions, is open to endless interpretation and manipulation, and may easily be misused in negotiations, or as an instrument for the reopening of political debates through law, thus weakening the fragile political processes of the Union. The potential for abuse, taking into account the constant interplay between Union law and 28 constitutional orders, whose own integrity and institutional quality varies, is immense in terms of probability. It would be in the interest of the national constitutional systems themselves to accept the risk of 'mishaps' from one single system (the Union system) rather than to live with the possibility of mistakes coming from 28 different systems. Indeed, pluralism not only endangers the integrity of Union law: it also endangers the integrity of the national rule of law, for Union law is part of it.

It is common sense that an overarching system should regulate its own relationship with the particular systems connected to it. If that regulation is left to each subsystem, a stochastic process of fragmentation would start sooner or later, its avoidance would be entrusted to sheer good will, and the whole idea of a common legal order would become unfeasible. The primacy of the shared system of law is indeed the logical solution we find in well-functioning divided-power systems. The truth is that there is no workable alternative. When more than one legal order may apply in a given situation, there has to be a rule saying—in a reasonably predictable manner—which one takes precedence in case of conflict. If the particular orders decide unilaterally on the relationship, always or in some undefined category of cases, the possibility of a common normative space will be slim and a matter of pure chance, and the process of fragmentation and decay a mere question of time.

From the perspective of historical experience and of the shared responsibility of the European states for integration, the approach of Union law to its relationship with national law is more *productive* and more *ordered* than those national or pluralist approaches that contest the autonomy and primacy of Union law, with damaging consequences for the rule of law in Europe. The preferable approach to the relationship between Union law and state law would be to count integration among the highest constitutional values—in Union law and also in national law. In consequence, the common legal order should not be limited by other values and principles. This means that national constitutional actors should play by the common rules and allow the Court of Justice to determine, within the sphere of Union law autonomously defined by that Court, the meaning and effects of that law.

From this perspective, the exceptional and mostly hypothetical resistance of some national constitutional courts to the primacy of Union law should be understood as a form of 'institutional disobedience'.[28] That disobedience disrupts the shared legal order and, by the same token, the national constitution and rule of law. It cannot be conceived of as an act in defence of the law or of the constitution. It is, as an instance of civil disobedience, an exceptional political act trespassing the boundaries of the legal system, but it might be legitimate, in extreme circumstances, if some conditions are respected. First, such a course of action may only be based on higher principles which command respect in all the systems concerned. Secondly, it should only be used as a last resort, after having used in good faith the mechanisms of the common system. Thirdly, it should be undertaken publicly and explicitly, not covertly. Finally, before proposing to use it national authorities should carefully analyse all the arguments from all sides, weigh the

[28] See Baquero Cruz, 'Legal Pluralism and Institutional Disobedience in the European Union', *supra* note 1.

general and particular advantages and disadvantages of breaching the common legal system, consider alternatives, and be willing to accept all the negative consequences of their action for the various levels concerned.

Perhaps those cases of exceptional disobedience are already framed, to a very large extent, by Union law itself. Indeed, Article 4(2) TEU provides the normative basis for a balancing between the fundamental structures of national constitutions and the essential principles of Union law, which include primacy, unity, effectiveness, sincere cooperation, and equality between the Member States. As regards fundamental rights, Article 53 of the Charter of Fundamental Rights of the European Union regulates the interplay between the level of protection provided by the Charter and the protection granted by other instruments, including the Member States' constitutions. It is for the Court of Justice to interpret and apply those provisions of Union law, including in the event of a preliminary reference from a national constitutional court. Concerning Article 4(2) TEU, in very exceptional cases in which the essence of a fundamental national constitutional structure is seriously compromised by Union law and the impact on the key principles and values of the Union is less intense, the Court of Justice could accept a special legal position for the Member State concerned, derogating from the normal application of Union law. In such cases, the ensuing fragmentation would have to be assessed by the political process, which could repair it through legal changes at national or Union level.

The existence of this mediating mechanism in Union law seems to leave very little space, if any, for the more disruptive unilateral defence of the state constitutions by national actors. Besides, in view of the degree of convergence between the fundamental values and principles of the European constitutional orders, and of the existence of a common legal culture, recourse to Article 4(2) TEU should be extremely unusual.

4

Somebody once wrote that we need false ideas because they are dynamic and generate movement, and that the greater the distance between reality and illusion, the more such ideas are anticipated, cherished, and followed by many, in their mythical unreality.

Constitutional pluralism was exactly this sort of false idea. It came. It stirred things up, proposing to subvert integration and the very structure of law. But its force is now spent. We should turn to something else.

That something else could be the task of rediscovering the law of integration, of exploring its unrealized potential and implications, and of understanding the conditions that make it possible, the grounds of its uncertain mode of being, the reasons for the difficulties it currently faces. The need to engage in it is underscored by a keen consciousness of the historical experience which led to integration and by its ongoing relevance today.

We may want to discuss the legitimacy of the law of integration and the content of Union policies; we may try to improve them (for they have defects and are perfectible); we may try to improve the accompanying institutional framework and decision-making processes, to reconsider the problematic design of the economic and monetary union, to establish mechanisms to redistribute more fairly the positive and negative economic consequences of integration, etc. But that does not have anything to do with constitutional pluralism. That discussion can and should take place as a matter of Union politics, without questioning the nature and basic structure of Union law. Unless we are convinced that integration is no longer useful and should be discarded, 'rolled back', or 'phased out'—if we still see it as a precious asset we have received in trust—then the original form of the law of integration should not be negotiable or traded against other things. It is there with its full value as a mechanism to integrate political communities, and to deal with endemic conflict in a civilized way.

4

THE PRELIMINARY RULINGS PROCEDURE: CORNERSTONE OR BROKEN ATLAS?

1

Following the insight of Pierre Pescatore, I have proposed that integration should be viewed as a complex assemblage of values, principles, rules, institutions, and powers—like elements that are interlinked through a number of wires or strings.[1] Those strings are the procedures foreseen by the Treaties. They hold the system together, allowing the figures to move and to change position. They connect the institutions, channelling their powers and allowing them to operate. Procedures such the Treaty revision procedure or the ordinary legislative procedure, with the particular role attributed to each actor taking part, shape the Union as much as other elements of the system, if not more. Procedures are thus essential to any correct understanding of the dynamics of integration, as they reflect the values and principles underlying it. In spite of their apparent dryness and dullness, much of the substance of integration is to be found in the procedures which give life to this complex mobile.

I have also argued that the Union has become what it is, to a very large extent, as a result of the deliberate choice to use the law as the means to formalize the relations between its states in a common autonomous organization, and also as a consequence of the decision to establish the Court of Justice instead of creating a softer dispute settlement mechanism such as an arbitral tribunal.

[1] For my previous ideas on the subject, see 'La procedure préjudicielle suffit-elle à garantir l'efficacité et l'uniformité du droit de l'Union européenne?', in L. Azoulai and L. Burgorgue-Larsen (eds.), *L'autorité de l'Union européenne* (2006) 241; 'De la cuestión prejudicial a la casación europea: Reflexiones sobre la eficacia y la uniformidad del Derecho de la Unión', *Revista española de Derecho Europeo* (2005) 35.

What's Left of the Law of Integration? Decay and Resistance in European Union Law. First Edition. Julio Baquero Cruz. Published 2018 by Oxford University Press.

Integration would not have developed the way it has without the law and the Court.

In turn, Union law and the Court of Justice would not be what they are without the preliminary rulings procedure. That procedure occupies a central position among all the other ways to bring cases to the Court. It also has a key position among all the procedures connecting institutions and framing the use of power in the Union. But to state its importance is not enough. We need to understand the reasons for its centrality in the system and explore its strengths and weaknesses. As with the other elements of the mobile of integration, this particular tool should be seen in a historical light. Its development and current state also bear witness to the promise and difficulties of integration, starting from the initial hopes, fuelled by historical consciousness, and leading to the current disaffection and blindness, and the attendant risks for its civilizational achievements.

2

The preliminary reference procedure is a unique bridge between the Court of Justice and national courts, allowing for an interaction between European Union law and the laws of the Member States. It is not just a connection between judicial bodies, but also between legal systems. As I have argued, direct effect, and to a large extent also primacy, are implicit in the preliminary reference procedure, the existence of which is a key structural argument in favour of both principles. This procedure shows that the law of integration was never meant to be confined to regulating relationships between the Member States.

This procedure is also one of the foundations for the autonomy of the European system, and one of the structures distinguishing it from standard international cooperation. Since it can be triggered by any judge in any Member State, with potential consequences for all the judges in all those states, and since those judges are independent national organs in view of the common constitutional principle of the separation of powers, the judicial process of the Union has always been autonomous from the transient will of the political organs of the Member States and also from the action or inaction of the Union institutions.

These remarks, however, reflect the knowledge we have about the way in which the preliminary rulings procedure was interpreted and used in practice. We need to grasp the significance it had when it was introduced, seeing it without the spectacles of experience. We have grown so used to it that we may no longer perceive the breakthrough of its insertion into the Treaties of Paris and Rome. In addition, it is difficult to separate the original provision from the interpretative choices made by the Court.

When the Treaties of Paris and Rome were concluded—as at present—traditional international agreements, generally understood as bilateral or multilateral instruments between the 'contracting parties', did not usually include their own dispute settlement system. Disputes would be solved through the means available under public international law. If such a system was foreseen, be it through arbitration or through an international court, it would normally deal with conflicts between sovereign states. When international courts or dispute settlement bodies were created, they had no connection with national courts and lived in perfect isolation. This disconnection was the institutional counterpart of the disconnection between legal systems. The international legal order and the national laws generally lived in separate normative worlds. The reception of international law in the national legal systems was often decided by each of the latter. In consequence, international law could not organize its effects effectively and uniformly. This was and remains one of the central reasons for the insufficient formalization of public international law.

It should come as no surprise, therefore, that one of the things the drafters of the Treaties of Paris and Rome did in their effort to overcome the shortcomings of the traditional framework of relationships between European nations, was to establish the Court of Justice and to connect it with national courts through a particular procedure. They rejected the simplest conceivable connection: an appeal before the Court, on grounds of the shared system of law, against decisions of the highest courts of the Member States. A European appeal was not considered, or if it was it was rejected, perhaps because it would have been excessively intrusive for national judicial structures, allowing the Court to set aside the decisions of national courts, and perhaps also as a system which could quickly become overburdened. An individual right of appeal was the connecting technique chosen in the context of the other main post-war supranational novelty, the European Convention of Human Rights with its Court. In the long run, that choice proved to have some advantages, but also several drawbacks: overburden, extremely long delays, and a normative connection of very low intensity between legal orders. The drafters of the Treaties of Paris and Rome opted for a different way, based on a dialogue between national courts and the common judicial body: the preliminary rulings procedure. The inspiration for that choice was constitutional and technical.

The constitutional genealogy becomes clear when the procedure is set in the framework of post-war legal and political reconstruction. Two Member States (Italy and Germany) had recently adopted constitutions with preliminary reference mechanisms on constitutional matters, on the assumption that the constitutional court would become the central and specialized jurisdiction for them, and that the procedure between courts would allow the new constitutional culture to irradiate the whole legal system without radically unsettling the previous structure of the national judiciary. In Germany an individual action for the protection of fundamental rights was added, while in Italy the correct application of the constitution by ordinary courts was exclusively entrusted to a system of preliminary references to the constitutional court.

The technical dimension of the choice becomes apparent when the procedure is compared with other preliminary procedures which are widely used in national legal orders in order to ensure consistency between decisions of the judges competent for each branch of the law. In accordance with such procedures, for example, some legal issues take priority and must be settled before a given case is disposed of, and this is commonly done through a preliminary reference procedure involving the competent national courts. Following a similar technique, the issues of the law of integration had to be settled by its specialized jurisdiction, the Court of Justice, in a binding decision, before a final judgment was issued by the national court dealing with a given case.

Those were the main models for the introduction of the preliminary rulings procedure of the Treaty establishing the European Coal and Steel Community of 1951. Article 41 of that Treaty provided as follows: 'The Court shall have sole jurisdiction to give preliminary rulings on the validity of acts of the High Authority and of the Council where such validity is in issue in proceedings brought before a national court or tribunal.'[2]

As already suggested, this kind of provision was unprecedented and to this day remains most unusual in public international law—in spite of less successful imitations in some systems of regional integration. The provision implies that the law of the European Coal and Steel Community would not be a purely internal law, exclusively administered, interpreted, and applied by the institutions of the Community. That provision only makes sense on the understanding that that law will interact with national law and institutions, that it will be relevant in litigation before national courts, that its validity could be contested before them, and that it will also be relevant in disputes between private parties and public authorities. This means, again, that the decisions of the High Authority or the Council could directly affect the legal position of private parties—not just those of the Member States.

Other interesting elements of this text are the exclusive jurisdiction granted to the European Court of Justice—comparable to the exclusive jurisdiction of state constitutional courts to decide on the constitutionality of national legislation—and the reference to the 'preliminary' character of the procedure ('*à titre préjudiciel*'), which, in the light of similar national procedures, meant that the national procedure would be suspended while the Court of Justice dealt with the question of validity referred to it, and that the latter's decision would bind the national court. The binding character of preliminary rulings is confirmed by the use of the verb '*statuer*' or, in the English text, of the expression 'to give preliminary *rulings*'. The initial Court of Justice was not established to give advisory opinions which would be freely

[2] The terse original French text reads as follows: '*La Cour est seule compétente pour statuer, à titre préjudiciel, sur la validité des délibérations de la Haute Autorité et du Conseil, dans le cas où un litige porté devant un tribunal national mettrait en cause cette validité.*'

assessed by the referring courts. Its rulings on the validity of the acts of the Coal and Steel Community were binding and final.

For all its clarity, three important things were not expressly settled in the provision.

The first was whether there was an obligation for all national courts to refer issues of validity to the Court. From the exclusive jurisdiction granted to it one could however deduce that national courts were not competent to decide on the validity of the acts of the High Authority or the Council, and that they were bound to refer those questions to the Court of Justice if they had doubts about their validity.

A second aspect which remained unclear was the consequences of a breach of the obligation to refer, especially if it led to a national decision declaring an act of secondary law invalid or inapplicable. It was unclear, in other words, whether the obligation to refer was a genuine legal obligation, endowed with adequate sanctions, or a softer requirement. Using structural interpretation, however, one could deduce that those decisions could not affect the validity of Community law, could have no consequences beyond the case in hand, and could lead to infringement proceedings under Article 88 of the Treaty of Paris.

A third aspect that the text did not settle was the position of individuals with regard to the obligation to refer, and whether they had a right for a reference to be made. However, the reference to questions of validity '*in issue in proceedings brought* before a national court or tribunal' could be interpreted to mean that the party questioning the validity of an act of the High Authority or of the Council was empowered to prompt the reference by making such a plea.

It is also essential to note that this first procedure was limited to issues of validity—in the same way as the constitutional preliminary procedures mentioned earlier were and remain limited to issues of constitutionality. Now, while all judicial proceedings involve more or less complex or trivial issues of interpretation, and validity issues always require an interpretation (and might indeed be resolved through it), most judicial proceedings involving the law of integration are not about its validity but about its interpretation and its consequences for national law. This meant that the procedure could ensure that the secondary law of the European Coal and Steel Community was not held to be invalid in some Member States while being valid in the remainder states, but it could never ensure uniform interpretation and effective application in all the states. This restriction greatly reduced the width of the bridge laid down between legal systems and courts, curtailing its potential.

Together with the narrow initial scope of integration, this restriction might have been one of the reasons for the limited impact of the preliminary reference procedure of the Coal and Steel Community. This also allows us to fully grasp the significance of the decision of the drafters of the Treaty of Rome to extend it to issues of interpretation. The common jurisdiction was to decide not only on the pressing but unusual cases in which the validity of Community law was at stake, but also on the more frequent issues of interpretation. This had two main consequences. First, it increased the possibilities for national courts to request preliminary rulings. Secondly, the procedure did not only ensure a centralized adjudication on the validity of Community law: it became a vehicle for its uniform interpretation and effective application in the Member States.

The drafters of the Treaty of Rome introduced other important changes in the procedure, giving it the shape we are familiar with.

The first one is the distinction between lower national courts, which were able but not bound to refer issues of Community law to the Court of Justice, and national courts of last resort, which were bound to do so ('that court or tribunal *shall bring the matter* before the Court of Justice'). At the same time, the drafters maintained the expression 'give *preliminary rulings*', confirming the obligation of national courts to wait for those rulings and respect them.

Secondly, the drafters distinguished between the Treaty, regarding which only questions of interpretation could be raised, and secondary law, on which both questions of interpretation and validity could be raised. This underlines the autonomy of the law of integration and the constitutional character of the Treaty, whose validity can never be contested, be it before the Court of Justice or before national courts.

Thirdly, the principle of the exclusive competence of the Court of Justice to rule on the validity and interpretation of Community law was no longer stated. This could be seen as a logical consequence of the distinction between lower courts and courts of last resort. Since lower courts had no obligation to refer, that competence could be thought to be shared between the Court of Justice and national courts. This seemed to imply that lower national courts were empowered to review the validity of acts of secondary law on their own and to declare them inapplicable—at least for the purpose of individual cases and subject to an appeal by the interested parties. As will be shown later, this interpretation was not followed by the Court.

The nature of the obligation to refer, the consequences and possible remedies following its breach, and the position of the parties to the national proceedings remained uncertain. In particular, the understanding of the procedure as an element of the right to effective judicial protection, whose breach could have consequences for the legality of national judicial decisions, was not clear—even though, as with Article 41 of the Treaty of Paris, the provision included interesting language.

Indeed, the second and third subparagraphs of Article 177 of the Treaty of Rome referred to a 'question *raised*'—and Article 267 of the Treaty on the Functioning of the European Union (TFEU) still does. That word could make one wonder: raised *by whom?* Generally, by the parties to the national proceedings or, exceptionally, by the national court of its own motion. In this regard, there is an intriguing textual difference between the second subparagraph of the provision, according to which the national court or tribunal *may* refer to the Court of Justice the issues of validity or interpretation raised before it *if it deems it necessary* in order to rule on the case, and the third subparagraph, for which a court of last resort is simply bound to refer such issues ('*est tenue de saisir*') without any assessment as to the necessity to have a preliminary ruling on them.

This 'historical' interpretation could suggest that the drafters intended to protect the position of the parties to the national case in subparagraph 3, so that whenever they raised such an issue before a national court of last resort, that court would be bound to refer. One could have thought that while lower national courts had unfettered discretion to assess *the necessity* of a preliminary ruling to give their judgment, courts of last resort—in view of their crucial position in the judicial system—would have no such discretion and would be bound to refer any issue of validity or interpretation of Community law raised before them. Ultimately, as we also know, this interpretation was not followed either.

Reading the relevant provisions while ignoring the case law which later construed them, one understands that those provisions, in the same way as other provisions of primary law, opened a vast interpretative field with a number of choices. A relationship between national courts and the Court of Justice had to be established, that was clear, as were some key elements of that relation, but some important aspects were less clear. Interpretation would have to flesh out the meaning of the provision, and especially the issues which are most crucial in structural terms: the position of the parties to the national proceedings and the contours of the obligation to refer.

3

These and other key aspects of the preliminary reference procedure were addressed by the Court in a series of judgments, which this section tries to summarize.

First, from the start the approach of the Court was based on a neat distinction between interpretation and application, and on a strict separation between the law of integration and national law. For the Court, the preliminary rulings procedure only allowed it to interpret Community law or to rule on its validity, not to apply that law or to meddle with national law. It was for the referring court to apply the Community rules as interpreted by the Court of Justice and to extract their consequences for national law.[3]

Secondly, the Court strongly protected the power of lower courts to refer from any interference by national procedural

[3] These distinctions are already present in *Van Gend en Loos*, at 10 and 22, and *Costa v. ENEL*, at 592 and 593 (both chapter 2, note 7).

law.[4] The case law on the obligation of courts of last resort to submit a preliminary reference is scant in comparison with that on the wide possibility for lower courts to refer. Through the engagement of lower courts, the preliminary rulings procedure became a dynamic element in spite of the hierarchical structures of the judiciaries of the Member States. In normal circumstances, lower national courts have to follow the case law of their higher courts. If they have a different view on a given legal issue, lower courts may try to change that case law, but their judgments are subject to review by the higher courts and may be quashed by them. The preliminary rulings procedure allowed lower courts to question the case law of higher courts, in tandem with the Court of Justice, in cases in which European law was applicable. The procedure thus became one of the main instruments allowing Union law to be a catalyst in the legal systems of the Member States, paving the way for changes that, in a purely national context, would probably have been blocked by entrenched legal cultures or by the underlying political and socio-economic forces.

Thirdly, although the text of the Treaty could have been read differently, the Court of Justice asserted a complete monopoly over issues of validity through structural interpretation, in view of its exclusive competence regarding actions for annulment, and concluded that 'national courts have no jurisdiction themselves to declare that acts of Community institutions are invalid'.[5]

Fourthly, the preliminary reference procedure was understood as a bilateral relationship between courts in which the parties had a very limited role. This is clearly expressed in *CILFIT*: 'Article [267 TFEU] *does not constitute a means of redress available to the parties* to a case pending before a national court or tribunal. Therefore, *the mere fact that a party contends that the dispute gives rise to a question concerning the interpretation of Community law does not mean that the court or tribunal concerned is compelled to consider that a question has been raised within the meaning of Article [267 TFEU]*'. 'On the other hand', the Court added, 'a national

[4] See, e.g., Case 166/73, *Rheinmühlen*, EU:C:1974:3.

[5] Case 314/85, *Foto-Frost*, EU:C:1987:452, at para. 20.

court or tribunal may, in any appropriate case, refer a matter to the Court of Justice *of its own motion*'.[6]

Fifthly, the requirement relating to the 'necessity' of a reference was held to apply to both subparagraphs of Article 267 TFEU, not only to issues of Community law raised before lower courts—disregarding the different drafting of both subparagraphs and discarding the interpretation mentioned earlier. The Court thus held that national courts of last resort have 'the same discretion as any other national court or tribunal to ascertain whether a decision on a question of Community law is necessary to enable them to give judgment'.[7] However, once those courts of last resort consider that recourse to Community law is 'necessary' to enable them to decide a case, Article 267 TFEU imposes on them *an obligation to refer*.[8]

Sixthly, the Court introduced three exceptions to that obligation. The first exception mentioned in *CILFIT* was taken from the *Da Costa* judgment of 1963: 'the authority of an interpretation under Article [267 TFEU] already given by the Court may deprive the obligation of its purpose and thus empty it of its substance. Such is the case especially when the question raised is materially identical with a question which has already been the subject of a preliminary ruling in a similar case.'[9] The second exception was an extension of the first one to cases in which 'previous decisions of the Court have already dealt with the point of law in question, irrespective of the nature of the proceedings which led to those decisions, even though the questions at issue are not strictly identical'.[10] These two exceptions are understandable, for in such cases a reference would be redundant, and the assessment of whether the question or the point of law has already been dealt with by the Court leaves very little discretion to national courts.

Finally, the Court also excluded the obligation to refer in cases in which 'the correct application of Community law [is] so

[6] Case 283/81, *CILFIT*, EU:C:1982:335, at para. 9 (emphasis added).

[7] *Ibid.*, at para. 10. [8] *Ibid.*, at para. 11.

[9] *Ibid.*, at para. 13, referring to Joined Cases 28 to 30/62, *Da Costa*, EU:C:1963:6.

[10] *Ibid.*, at para. 14.

obvious as to leave no scope for any reasonable doubt as to the manner in which the question raised is to be resolved'. The Court strictly framed this exception:

> Before it comes to the conclusion that such is the case, the national court or tribunal must be convinced that the matter is equally obvious to the courts of the other Member States and to the Court of Justice. Only if those conditions are satisfied, may the national court or tribunal refrain from submitting the question to the Court of Justice and take upon itself the responsibility for resolving it.

The possibility of not making a reference had to be assessed in the light of the specific features of Community law, including its multilingual character, the special terminology used by that law, and its own methods of interpretation, with the special emphasis it generally puts on contextual and teleological interpretation.[11]

It is tempting to see *CILFIT* as a statement about the relationship between national courts of last resort and the Court of Justice, a statement that would deny any role to the parties to the national case, leaving them at the complete mercy of the decision of the national court. A closer look, however, may allow us to unearth a meaning of *CILFIT* that does not ignore the position of the parties. At bottom, the judgment is also about the 'responsibility' of judging, a crucial function for the protection of the underlying substantive rights and for the fundamental right to an effective judicial protection.

In the text of the relevant Treaty provision, a clear, precise, and unconditional obligation to refer is addressed to national courts of last resort, which are organs of the Member States. The provision therefore would seem to meet the conditions to have direct effect, giving rise to an individual right to a preliminary

[11] *Ibid.*, at paras. 16–20. It has been argued that two recent judgments of the second chamber of the Court have 'recalibrated' the *acte clair* doctrine, granting 'much greater freedom' to national courts of last resort (see Kornezov, 'The New Format of the *Acte Clair* Doctrine and its Consequences', 53 *Common Market Law Review* (2016) 1317, referring to Case C-160/14, *Ferreira da Silva*, EU:C:2015:565 and Joined Cases C-72/14 and C-197/14, *X v. Inspecteur van Rijksbelastingdienst*, EU:C:2015:564). This claim might seem odd, as a five-judge chamber of the Court could not modify case law that has remained untouched for more than three decades.

reference by those courts. In point of fact, the Court never denied the existence of such an effect and of the corresponding right. It only stated that the preliminary reference procedure was not 'a means of redress', i.e. a remedy that the parties could trigger automatically, in the same way they trigger an appeal. Those limited statements do not exclude the existence of an individual right, which would be the counterpart of the legal obligation to refer imposed on national courts of last resort. In *CILFIT* the Court confirmed the existence of that obligation, subject to certain conditions and exceptions. That obligation should not be seen as a simple duty *towards the system*—a duty of sincere cooperation devoid of consequences for individuals. It may also be understood as an obligation towards the party arguing that the obligation to refer applies in a particular case. Within the bounds of those conditions and exceptions, that party would thus have an individual right for a reference to be made. The fundamental right to effective judicial protection, now enshrined in Article 47 of the Charter of Fundamental Rights of the Union, lends support to this interpretation.

It may thus be misleading to consider that in *CILFIT* the Court of Justice blindly entrusted the correct functioning of the preliminary rulings mechanism, whose structure is completed by the obligation to refer, to the goodwill of national courts of last resort. Those courts were never meant to have an absolute discretion to refer or not to refer. Their responsibility in taking that procedural step is strictly framed, excluding arbitrariness and implying that they are not the only judges of their own obligation. The only thing the Court left open in *CILFIT* was the question of the remedies the system could offer if there is a breach of the obligation to refer, i.e. in case of judicial decisions leading to structural failure.

4

The preliminary reference procedure, as fleshed out by the Court throughout decades of judicial practice, has many advantages, but it also has a number of weaknesses. It is essential to understand those weaknesses in order to assess the role of the procedure in the system of integration and its current state of health. At present, with so many Member States and in view of the very wide scope and depth of Union law, it could be wondered whether that mechanism is still the best tool to ensure the uniform and effective interpretation of that law across the vast judicial space of the Union.

A first weakness has to do with the risk, inherent in the distinction between *interpretation* and *application*, of diluting the responsibility of judging in the dialogue between the Court of Justice and national courts, potentially undermining a central function of judicial adjudication. Here 'flexibility', generally perceived as a positive trait of the procedure, may become problematic.

The distinction between interpretation and application has always been at the heart of the Court's conception of the preliminary rulings procedure. In all the other judicial procedures before the Union Courts this distinction does not play a role, as those Courts must adjudicate in full the cases brought to them—for example, by annulling an act subject to an action for annulment or by dismissing the action, or by awarding damages or refusing them in an action for damages. In the procedure laid down in Article 267 TFEU, that distinction is as difficult to trace in practice as it is unsustainable as a matter of theory. The application of a legal provision in a concrete factual situation always presupposes its interpretation, which may be more or less complex or, sometimes, completely uncontroversial. Conversely, the meaning of a legal provision is only elucidated, and its interpretation brought to completion, once all its consequences for a particular case are clearly spelled out—i.e. through its application. Legal interpretation is not limited to the general elaboration of the content of a provision. Its concrete consequences for a case are part—often the most important part—of the seamless process of judicial interpretation and adjudication. The distinction between interpretation and application, the quicksand on which the preliminary reference procedure is supposed to be built, opens an ambiguous space in the judicial process of the Union, a space that could be excessively vague for the parties and for justice.

This distinction allows the Court of Justice to modulate quite freely, on a case by case basis, the normative content of its judgments and the part it takes—or does not take—in the responsibility of judging, which it shares with the national court. In some cases the Court may take extremely thin or 'poor' judicial decisions, entrusting the national judge with the assessment of whether a national measure is 'proportionate' in the light of fairly scant guidance.

Among several examples of judgments of this kind, let me recall a rather extreme one. In *Freiburger Kommunalbauten* the referring court, the *Bundesgerichtshof* of Germany, asked the Court of Justice whether a particular contractual term was unfair within the meaning of Article 3(1) of Directive 93/13.[12] About two years later the Court sent back the following answer: 'It is for the national court to decide whether a contractual term such as that at issue in the main proceedings satisfies the requirements for it to be regarded as unfair under Article 3(1) of [Directive 93/13].' The guidance given by the Court in the body of the judgment was meagre to say the least.

In other cases, by contrast, the Court may decide Union law issues in a very clear-cut manner, leaving little or nothing to be decided by the referring judge, and seemingly ignoring its own distinction between interpretation and application. For example, although the application of the criteria for establishing state liability for breaches of Union law is generally left to the competent national court, in *Köbler* the Court stated that it had 'all the materials enabling it to establish whether the conditions necessary for liability of the Member State to be incurred [were] fulfilled', and it went on to adjudicate the case in full.[13]

Most of the time the Court will stay somewhere between these two extremes, giving a measure of guidance to the national court but also some leeway regarding the final decision, i.e. not providing a conclusive interpretation. In some cases this flexibility may be problematic, for a number of reasons.

First of all, with thin or 'poor' judgments Union law remains more or less open and not totally interpreted—only half-interpreted, half-cooked, as it were. Frequently it is not clear

[12] Case C-237/02, *Freiburger Kommunalbauten*, EU:C:2004:209, at para. 14; Council Directive 93/13 on unfair terms in consumer contracts, OJ 1993 L 95/29.

[13] Case C-224/01, *Köbler*, EU:C:2003:513, at para. 101.

what the referring judge will do with the preliminary ruling, and what will be the ensuing position of the parties. This may lead to problems of legal certainty, since those parties will not know what Union law means for them until the national judge completes the interpretative task left unfinished by the Court, which could lead to arbitrary interventions. When read carefully, thin preliminary rulings do not really look like *rulings*. They look more like sketchy legal advice that national courts should consider when taking their decisions—whereas pursuant to Article 267 TFEU the Court is supposed to take 'a *decision* on the question', 'to give a *ruling* thereon'. Besides, the precedential value of thin preliminary judgments is hazy. One judge, whether in the same or in another Member State, may read them in one way and another judge in another way. Thin preliminary rulings potentially lead to a reduction of the meaning and significance of Union law, and also to its fragmentation, betraying the main objective of the preliminary reference procedure and the very spirit of the law of integration.

Secondly, with preliminary rulings of this kind the main function of judicial adjudication may not be properly fulfilled. The essence of that function lies in deciding cases and establishing legal positions—rights and obligations. By adjudicating on such claims after following the steps of a procedure and giving reasons for their decisions, judicial bodies render the law more precise. A series of interconnected judgments traces finer lines than those of the applicable legal texts, classifying situations under this or that category. Judicial adjudication thus tends to draw a normative map on a much smaller scale than the grand map defined by legal provisions. With thin preliminary rulings, however, that finer map of legal positions will not be achieved, and the meaning of Union law will not be rendered as precise as it could become through a more rigorous use of the procedure.

Finally, the national court may doubt whether the reference was really useful. Waiting for a year or more to receive an inconclusive judgment must be a very frustrating experience for a national judge who played by the rules and expected a more nutritious answer. A one-year long procedure may not seem too lengthy when compared with national judicial proceedings if it brings real added value, adjudicating in a clear way the issues of Union law which were raised and bringing the case very close to the point of decision, but it will appear extremely lengthy if the Union law issues remain more or less undecided. If the national court, which may be of last resort, receives a thin judgment, next time it might think twice before sending a reference.

Sometimes the Court of Justice may not be able to avoid sending back to the referring court a Union legal issue which is not completely decided, as the consequences for the actual case may depend on factual assessments that the national judge is better placed to carry out, or on issues of national law that the Court is not competent to settle. In some cases, however, the impression given is that the relevant point of Union law is not left open for those reasons, but to facilitate the Court's task by sticking to uncontroversial legal questions while avoiding the hard ones.

There might be, indeed, an important, if questionable, institutional dimension to thin preliminary rulings.

They may be connected, firstly, to the tendency of the Court to write preliminary rulings as if they were a sort of 'judicial legislation'. As in other systems, there is pressure in the Union for its higher court to settle the questions left open by the compromises of the legislative process. The Court is able to cope with that pressure because its decision-making process, facilitated by shared legal methods, precedent, and simple majority voting, probably works more smoothly than the legislative process of the Union. But the Court may sometimes be tempted to perform that role of 'interstitial legislature' by rendering abstract judgments that do not really dispose of Union law issues, standing somewhere between legislation and standard judicial adjudication.

A second institutional function may be that of easing compromise between the judges deciding a case, releasing them from the 'anxiety' of having to take hard decisions or to outvote their fellow judges. Thin preliminary rulings also help to ensure a greater degree of 'coherence' between judgments in different cases and between chambers, to ensure acceptability by national courts and to avert constitutional conflicts. If precedents are thin, they will be easier to 'follow' for all the actors concerned.

A third reason for the increasing use of this kind of judgments may be the situation created by the rejection of the idea of a smaller Court with a stable composition. Today, the Court is composed of 28 judges, perhaps too many to allow it to maintain a strong and coherent voice. The most important cases are generally decided by the Grand Chamber, composed of 15 members who, with the exception of two (the President and the Vice-President of the Court), change for each case assigned to that Chamber. Majorities may shift as a result, especially in cases concerning sensitive issues. The thin or poor case law may be a device allowing the Court to 'agree with itself' throughout time in this complex institutional situation. But the price paid for this may be too dear.

5

Other significant weaknesses of the preliminary rulings procedure are its ambiguous nature and the ensuing suboptimal practice of national courts of last resort.

According to a widespread view, that procedure is based on a purely *voluntary* cooperation between free and equal judicial bodies. Trevor Hartley thus stated that it 'puts the European Court in a weaker position than the supreme court in a federation'; '[i]t suggests that the national courts are not subordinate to the European Court, but co-equal: the relationship is not one of hierarchy, but of co-operation'.[14] Joseph Weiler also characterized the constitutional dialogue in the Union 'as a conversation of many actors in a constitutional interpretive community, rather than as a hierarchical structure with the ECJ at the top'.[15] For some, this conversation could also take place outside the procedure, in informal exchanges between disconnected decisions in which national courts interact with the Court of Justice without actually engaging with it through preliminary references. This conception of the procedure as a flexible and soft mechanism will recall the ideas of the pluralists, their abhorrence of hierarchy, and their preference for

[14] Hartley, *The Foundations of European Community Law* (2nd edn. 1988) 246.
[15] Weiler, chapter 2, note 17, at 322.

open-ended and informal processes of accommodation. It will also be welcome by those who consider the nation state as the predominant political organization in contemporary Europe.

This conception, however, contradicts the terms of Article 267 TFEU and the central objective of integration: formalizing the relationships between the Member States in a predictable and effective legal framework. Seeing the procedure as a soft tool opens a space of potential normlessness in the cornerstone of the law of integration, endangering the whole edifice.

The Court may have contributed to this view with its own references to 'judicial cooperation', a term that could be misguiding if taken too literally. While it includes clear elements of cooperation, the preliminary rulings procedure is not always voluntary. In accordance with the third subparagraph of Article 267 TFEU, 'a court or tribunal of a Member State against whose decisions there is no judicial remedy under national law . . . *shall* bring the matter before the Court'. The aim of this obligation is that of preventing 'a body of national case law not in accord with the rules of Community law from coming into existence in any Member State'.[16] The obligation to refer subsists, with well-framed exceptions, and there is an obligation to respect preliminary rulings. Hence, although there is no 'European appeal' and national courts are not formally subordinated to the Court, the system is not based on a purely voluntary cooperation.

If the procedure worked as it is supposed to work, all issues of validity of Union law should be referred to the Court in case of doubt, and all issues of interpretation should be sent to it by courts of last resort unless they are irrelevant, already solved, or if the answer is manifestly obvious in accordance with the conditions laid down in *CILFIT*. Once the Court had determined those issues, its judgments would have to be respected by national courts throughout the Union. If the procedure were strictly complied with, the Court would determine all issues of Union law raised before national courts of last resort, and those national courts could never establish an autonomous

[16] Case 107/76, *Hoffmann-La Roche*, EU:C:1977:89, at para. 5.

national jurisprudence on them. While this situation does not create an institutional hierarchy between courts, it creates a structural relationship between national courts of last resort and the Court of Justice, a relationship that is based on a priority for the Court of Justice and a subordination of national courts when it comes to determining the validity or the meaning of Union law.

It is therefore more accurate to consider, with Pierre Pescatore, that this procedure, 'the true innovation of the Treaty of Rome', creates 'an organic link' between national courts and the Court.[17]

At the same time it cannot be denied that the Court has put a lot of trust on national courts, delegating to them decisions that can be essential for the proper functioning of the system. This trust, embodied in the word 'cooperation', may not always be warranted. As I have already suggested, sometimes the procedure is not used when and as it should, with the consequence that Union law is not always applied correctly or at all. Some preliminary references which should be made by national courts of last resort are not made. The degree of compliance varies among the Member States, but it is far from exemplary in many of them. Taking into account the width and depth of Union law at present, if *CILFIT* were respected in its own terms, or even in a softer version, the Luxembourg Court would be flooded with preliminary references. It is very likely that the Court only deals with part of the preliminary questions it should be dealing with, insofar as questions from courts of last resort are concerned. This could lead, and in some cases has led, to a multiplication of preliminary references from lower courts. An important part of the judicial application of Union law remains invisible, as the hidden part of an iceberg.

The way the system works does not seem to be optimal from the perspective of the primacy, uniformity, and effectiveness of Union law—the central aims of the preliminary rulings procedure. This might give the impression that the Member States

[17] Pescatore, chapter 1, note 3, at 73 and 82: '*lien organique*'; '*la véritable innovation du traité de Rome*'.

recover, through administrative and judicial autonomy, part of the freedom they seem to lose when the Union legislature adopts secondary law.

It could be argued that the absence of a preliminary reference from a national court of last resort is never a problem in itself, only when it leads to an incorrect interpretation of a substantive provision of Union law, which determines the legal position of the persons concerned. This view is questionable, since the preliminary rulings procedure has a direct impact on the legal position of individuals insofar as their rights to effective judicial protection are concerned. By not sending a preliminary reference when one should have been sent, national courts of last resort will already have breached a fundamental provision of Union law, even if they reach the correct solution on the merits—which would be difficult to verify in the absence of a judgment from the Court of Justice on the relevant issue. That omission is an autonomous breach of an essential procedural requirement, which cannot remain without consequences for the individual concerned. Besides, very often that breach will be accompanied by an incorrect interpretation of a substantive provision of Union law.

6

The main weakness of the preliminary rulings procedure lies in the perceived absence of a sanction for breaches of the obligation to refer that is imposed on national courts of last resort. A legal obligation generally presupposes a mechanism of enforcement, without which one cannot speak of a genuine obligation. It would be paradoxical if the central mechanism for the judicial application of Union law lacked an effective sanction. Union law is characterized by its autonomous legal force, which can be invoked by individuals before national courts and override national law in case of conflict. It would also be odd to leave the mechanism for the enforcement of rights based on Union law entirely in the hands of national judges of last resort. The *right of rights*, the action through which rights may be enforced, would depend on the discretion of those judges. The obligation to refer would thus be ‘essentially unenforceable'.[18] This possible structural defect in the construction of Union law could seriously undermine the direct effect and primacy of its substantive rules.

Although no perfect closure exists or may exist in the preliminary reference procedure, and only a European appeal would provide such a closure, the obligation to refer is not completely unenforceable. The Union system offers a number of resources to tackle problems of this kind.

The first tool that comes to mind is a subsequent reference from a lower court on the same point of law. This will not have an effect for a case decided at last instance without a reference, as that judgment would normally be *res judicata*, but a new reference remains possible and may allow the Court to prevent the crystallization of a line of case law of a national supreme court which is in breach of Union law. This means that the structural consequences of a breach of the obligation to refer are not as grave as one might think, since an incorrect judgment of a national court of last resort is not set in stone. On the other hand, that kind of intervention by lower national courts and the Court of Justice unsettles national judicial structures. In practice, it would always be preferable that national courts of last resort abide by their obligation to refer.

A second tool could be the infringement procedure of Article 258 TFEU. Any single breach of the obligation to refer constitutes a breach of Union law, and the Commission could initiate infringement proceedings for that reason. This remedy is, however, subject to serious practical limitations.

First, it will not affect the final character of the judgment of the national court of last resort in question, and it will not be a remedy for the individual affected by it, unless the judgment of the Court of Justice is later used as a basis to claim damages from the Member State. At the same time, a judgment declaring the infringement would bind the national authorities to intervene in order to render the national legal situation compatible with Union law.

[18] Kornezov, see note 11, at 1333.

Secondly, the Commission is not bound to initiate infringement proceedings even when it receives a complaint: it has full discretion to decide whether to initiate them or not. A person who is affected by a decision not to refer cannot force the Commission to initiate proceedings against the state concerned.[19]

Thirdly, even though infringement proceedings could be envisaged concerning systemic problems regarding the obligation to refer in this or that Member State, that avenue is not an appropriate remedy for individual breaches. The Commission might not have sufficient resources to deal with all those cases, and it would be quite difficult to select them in a consistent manner. From the point of view of an efficient use of its resources, it seems correct not to start infringement proceedings for single breaches of the obligation to refer.

Infringement proceedings could, however, be appropriate as regards systemic breaches of that obligation. For example, in what remains an isolated case, the Commission once started infringement proceedings against Sweden in view of the very limited number of preliminary references from its courts of last resort and of national procedural rules and practices that made it very difficult to obtain those references. The infringement proceedings were discontinued after Sweden adopted new procedural rules that, in the Commission's view, facilitated preliminary references from Swedish courts of last resort.[20]

A third tool could be the *Köbler* line of case law. In that judgment, the Court confirmed that the Member States are also bound to repair the harm caused to individuals in breach of Union law, if certain conditions are met, when the harm is due to decisions of their courts of last resort.[21] However, the conditions established by the Court mean that this remedy could only be used in limited cases.

[19] See, e.g., Case 247/87, *Star Fruit Company v. Commission*, EU:C:1989:58, at para. 11.

[20] For details, see U. Bernitz, 'The Duty of Supreme Courts to Refer Cases to the ECJ: The Commission's Action Against Sweden', in N. Wahl and P. Cramér (eds.), *Swedish Studies in European Law* volume 1 (2006) 37.

[21] *Köbler*, see note 13.

First, it is only available when the rule of law breached is 'intended to confer rights on individuals'.[22] Although the Court has not taken a position on this point, its case law does not seem to consider the obligation to refer as such a rule, since 'non-compliance by the court in question with its obligation' is only one of the factors to be taken into account when assessing whether a breach of Union law has occurred.[23] The Court sees the obligation to refer as a purely instrumental procedural rule whose breach could only be relevant for state liability if it leads to the infringement of a substantive provision of Union law.

Secondly, not all breaches will engage state liability. In the case law related to infringements due to other branches of the Member States, breaches must be 'sufficiently serious', which is a very high threshold. When the breach is due to a decision of a national court of last resort, an even more stringent standard is used: state liability 'can be incurred only *in the exceptional case where the court has manifestly infringed the applicable law*'.[24] This has to be assessed in the light of a number of factors, including, besides possible non-compliance with the obligation to refer, 'the degree of clarity and precision of the rule in question, whether the infringement was intentional, whether the error of law was excusable or inexcusable, the position taken, where applicable, by a Community institution',[25] or the 'manifest breach of the case law of the Court in the matter'.[26]

As with the general liability regime, the Member States may provide for less strict conditions and are required to extend to claims based on Union law the more favourable conditions which may exist for comparable domestic claims.[27] In the absence of such a regime, however, the *Köbler* remedy will only be available in very limited cases. Indeed, even in the case in hand, where the national court grossly misread a previous judgment of the Court, liability was not recognized and Mr Köbler did not obtain reparation for past damages—while

[22] *Ibid.*, at para. 51. [23] *Ibid.*, at para. 55.
[24] *Ibid.*, at para. 53 (emphasis added). [25] *Ibid.*, at para. 55.
[26] *Ibid.*, at para. 56. [27] *Ibid.*, at para. 57 and 58.

his administrative situation had to be revised for the future to comply with the Court's findings.[28]

In summary, *Köbler* offers a weak remedy for breaches of the obligation to refer. More than a decade after the judgment, the Court has only given a handful of additional preliminary rulings on this matter.[29] Although there is no comprehensive information about its use by national courts, a recent study refers to 35 reported cases in the whole European Union since 2003, with an award of damages in only four of them.[30]

This narrow path could be rendered a bit more useful if, as suggested above, the obligation to refer which is enshrined in Article 267 TFEU were considered as a directly effective rule conferring rights on individuals. The remedy would thus protect the integrity of the preliminary rulings procedure in its own right, at least in some cases, by allowing individuals to seek compensation for the damage caused by the absence of a reference, regardless of whether it led or not to the breach of a substantive provision of Union law.[31] Nevertheless, the path would remain narrow as regards the substantive test laid down by the Court. While a softer standard could lead to a more rigorous practice of the preliminary rulings procedure, such a test would bring the remedy very close to a sort of indirect appeal, unsettling national judicial structures and procedures. Non-contractual liability should be available, allowing redress to be obtained in the hopefully limited number of cases in which something has gone clearly wrong in the judicial process, but it is not an adequate sanction for all breaches of the obligation to refer.

[28] See para. 125: 'that reply [i.e. that the breach was not considered to be "manifest in nature and thus as sufficiently serious"] is without prejudice to the obligations arising for the Member State concerned from the Court's reply to the third question referred [i.e. the declaration that the Austrian case law was in breach of Union law].'

[29] Case C-173/03, *Traghetti del Mediterraneo*, EU:C:2006:391; Case C-160/14, *Ferreira da Silva*, EU:C:2015:565; Case C-168/15, *Tomášová*, EU:C:2016:602.

[30] Varga, 'Why is the *Köbler* Principle not Applied in Practice?', *Maastricht Journal of European and Comparative Law* (2016) 984, at 988.

[31] For a similar view, see Kornezov, see note 11, at 1340 and 1341.

The fourth possible tool, and probably the most promising one, is the protection of the fundamental right to an effective judicial protection through the procedures of national law and in the framework of the European Convention on Human Rights. This possibility is based on the reasonable understanding that the absence of a preliminary reference from national courts of last resort may, under certain conditions, breach the individual right to effective judicial protection.

As a matter of national law, a number of constitutional courts have already held that the refusal of a national court of last resort to send a reference to the Court of Justice could be in breach of the national fundamental right to effective judicial protection.[32] Once again, this remedy is not without shortcomings.

First, in most Member States this line of case law does not exist, and in some of them it is difficult to conceive, as there is no specialized jurisdiction or remedy for the protection of fundamental rights. Secondly, in those states in which the remedy exists the examples are isolated and do not show a frequent and vigorous review of the obligation to refer. Thirdly, in this line of case law only the national fundamental right is protected, not the right enshrined in Article 47 of the Charter. Finally, the criteria and the corresponding standard of protection vary from state to state, and do not coincide with those according to which a national court is bound to refer under Union law. The protection granted is thus exogenous to the Union system, not uniform, infrequent, and not provided as a matter of Union law.

A similar remedy exists before the Strasbourg Court on the basis of Article 6 of the European Convention on Human Rights. In that context, there is a well-established line of case law according to which the refusal by a national court of last resort to make a preliminary reference may infringe the fairness

[32] Such case law exists at least in Austria, Belgium, the Czech Republic, Germany, Slovakia, Slovenia, and Spain. For details, see Lacchi, 'Review by Constitutional Courts of the Obligation of National Courts of Last Instance to Refer a Preliminary Question to the Court of Justice of the EU', 16(6) *German Law Journal* (2016) 1663.

of proceedings if it is an arbitrary decision, i.e. not duly justified with regard to the requirements of Article 267 TFEU.[33]

This latter remedy could be very effective in reinforcing the position of individuals and framing the practice of national courts of last resort. It has the advantages of being available in all the Member States which are party to the Convention and subject to the jurisdiction of the European Court of Human Rights, and of referring to the requirements of Article 267 TFEU, protected through Article 6 of the Convention. But this avenue is not without its drawbacks: the slowness of the procedure before the Strasbourg Court; the fact that it is external to the Union's system and disconnected from the Charter; and the risk that the Strasbourg Court may limit itself to checking whether sufficient grounds were given about the obligation to refer, as a purely formal matter, without reviewing the correctness of those grounds.

These interesting developments at national level and in the framework of the European Convention on Human Rights invite us to reflect about their possible consequences for the Union legal order. Once the Union accedes to the Convention, as it is bound to do, Article 6 thereof, with its content regarding the obligation to refer, will become part of the Union legal order. Even before accession takes place, Article 52(3) and (4) of the Charter of Fundamental Rights provide that the interpretation of Article 47 of the Charter, on the right to effective judicial protection, shall be harmonious with the constitutional traditions common to the Member States, and cannot be less protective than the Convention.

7

This overview of the structural strengths and weaknesses of the preliminary rulings procedure, and of the possible remedies to

[33] See, among others, ECtHR, *Ullens de Schooten and Rezabek v. Belgium*, Appl. nos. 3989/07 and 38353/07, judgment of 20 September 2011; ECtHR, *Vergauwen and others v. Belgium*, Appl. no. 4832/04, judgment of 10 April 2012; and *Schipani and others v. Italy*, Appl. no. 38369/09, judgment of 21 July 2015. (All ECtHR decisions are available online at http://hudoc.echr.coe.int/.)

breaches of the obligation to refer, shows the paradoxical position of that procedure in the system of integration. It is obviously better than nothing, as it allows Union law to have a life of its own in the national legal orders, and a degree of effectiveness and uniformity that is not seen in more traditional international legal instruments. At the same time, its erratic performance means that its potential is not used to its full extent and that those objectives are not sufficiently achieved.

It is tempting to say—and there might be some truth in saying—that the variable but overall suboptimal performance of the preliminary rulings procedure is due to the deficient internalization of Union law in national legal cultures, and to the weakness of the shared European legal culture. If national legal actors do not view themselves as actors within a wider legal and institutional system and do not use the tools of that system, which they perceive as an essentially foreign object, then it is only natural that the preliminary rulings procedure is not always used when and as it should, and that Union law is not always applied when and as it should. If those actors consistently behaved as actors of the Union system, and used the resources of that system when they had to, legal practice would come much closer to the normative requirements of the law of integration.

That view, however, reifies legal culture and ignores the fact that legal and institutional devices can act upon that culture, transforming it. The suboptimal performance of the preliminary reference mechanism may be due, at least in part, to problems of design or interpretation unconnected to national legal cultures and may be remedied without any prior change in those cultures.

More than a decade ago, I explored what I then considered a more perfect solution for the interaction between national courts and the Court of Justice: an appeal before the latter, on points of Union law, against decisions taken by national courts of last resort.[34] This device would have a number of advantages, but it would also have many disadvantages.

[34] See the articles mentioned *supra* note 1.

A first advantage would be that of offering a clear closure to the judicial system of the Union and an adequate remedy for the parties to cases in which Union law is applicable. In such a system, the final judicial decision would no longer depend on the autonomous decision of a national court of last resort to send a reference to the Court of Justice, but on the possibility granted to each party of challenging national judicial decisions. If access to the Court of Justice is part of the right to an effective legal protection enshrined in Article 47 of the Charter, such a system would clearly offer a more robust protection of that right.

Secondly, a Union appeal would also have the advantage of allowing part of the hidden mass of the iceberg of the judicial application of Union law to emerge, limiting its underground application and its relative invisibility.

Finally, a Union appeal would discipline the Court of Justice itself in its sometimes dubious use of the flexibility of the preliminary reference system. As suggested above, an appeal must be decided: it should be dismissed or lead to the full or partial annulment of the decision under review. It binds the Court, therefore, to determine the issues of Union law raised by the party lodging the appeal. The Court of Justice would not be able to refrain from exercising part of its judicial function and from tracing the more detailed normative map generally expected from case law.

There are, nevertheless, important objections to such a far-reaching change. The first, of course, is that it is not realistic in political terms. The present Union and its Member States do not seem to have much appetite to advance further in the path of integration. The probability that a Union appeal will be adopted, let alone discussed, by the Member States in a future reform of the Treaties is close to zero.

A second objection to a Union appeal would be that the Court could end up like the Strasbourg Court, crushed beneath thousands of appeals, deciding cases after procedures lasting many years, and with an ever increasing backlog. A European appeal would thus lead to an even less efficient system than the current one. This objection, however, is easily countered: in such a case the Union system of courts should be changed. The Court could have more judges if the Treaties were modified.

The General Court is in the process of doubling its members. A decentralized and more developed judicial structure could also be considered. Or the Court could be granted the power to select which cases to decide, through a filter system.

There is a more solid argument for opposing the introduction of a European appeal and in favour of maintaining the preliminary reference procedure, and this has to do with the institutional and legal architecture of the Union. In the Union, the central level has very limited functions. Only in a few areas does the Union have a central administration, taking binding decisions (competition, state aid, etc.). In those areas there is a system of centralized judicial review (General Court and appeals before the Court). In other areas it is for the Member States to apply Union law through their own administrations, in a decentralized manner, and to provide for judicial review before their courts.

Seen from this perspective, the current system, in which national courts bear the burden of reviewing most of the decentralized application of Union law, while the Union Courts only intervene when direct actions are possible or through the preliminary rulings procedure, fits better with the institutional realities of the Union than would a European appeal. Such an appeal could, however, work in a system with a clearer separation between Union law and national law, and endowed with a more developed Union administration.

The fact that the preliminary rulings procedure is the device which fits best with the current Union institutional and legal realities does not mean that it cannot be improved. As already suggested, its potential is, perhaps, yet to be fully realized, many decades after its introduction. Improvements are clearly possible.

On the one hand, the Court should reflect on its own practice, in particular about the need to provide real added value to the referring court, to determine with an acceptable degree of legal certainty the consequences of Union law for each case, and to fulfil the judicial task of drawing, case by case, a more detailed normative map.

On the other hand, more attention should be paid to the 'joint' where the system often 'cracks': the obligation on national courts of last resort to refer. After reviewing the available but imperfect remedies against breaches of this obligation, one can conclude that in a preliminary reference procedure a remedy providing for perfect closure will never be available. At the same time, the potential of those imperfect avenues is not sufficiently used. Among all of them, considering the procedure as part of the fundamental right to effective judicial protection seems the most promising one. However, the protection provided by national courts should be granted as a matter of Union law and in accordance with it, and the system of the European Convention on Human Rights should only come into play as a very last remedy.

This requires some interpretative efforts. The first challenge is to connect the obligation to refer with the right to effective judicial protection enshrined in Article 47 of the Charter. That a connection exists is clear in some judgments of the Court of Justice.[35] The connection, however, should go beyond a purely structural link. Following the case law of some national constitutional courts and of the Strasbourg Court, the Court of Justice should flesh out the position of the individual in the preliminary reference procedure on the basis of Article 47 of the Charter. As already suggested, the obligation to refer could give rise to direct effect and deserves as much protection as any substantive provision of Union law, especially if it is part of the effective judicial protection granted by Article 47 of the Charter.

The second challenge is to find an adequate enforcement mechanism for the normative consequences of the combined interpretation of Article 267 TFEU and Article 47 of the Charter. Union law does not provide for a specific action for the protection of the fundamental rights granted by the Charter, but in accordance with Article 19(1) TEU (and settled case law) the Member States are bound to establish effective and equivalent remedies for the protection of legal positions based on Union law. The applicability of Article 47 of the Charter is beyond doubt: when the Member States establish remedies for the protection of Union rights, they do so within the scope of Union law, pursuant to the obligation laid down in Article 19(1) TEU. If the obligation to refer is correctly seen as part of the

[35] Case C-506/04, *Wilson*, EU:C:2006:587, at paras. 47 and 48; and Case C-72/15, *Rosneft*, EU:C:2017:236.

effective judicial protection required by Article 47 of the Charter, then the Member States should provide for remedies which are at least equivalent to those available under national law for breaches of equivalent rules. When the obligation to refer is at issue, the national procedures for the protection of fundamental rights should be open for claims based on Article 47 of the Charter—and not on the equivalent national right, which would not be applicable in such situations, as Union law fully determines the scope of the obligation to refer and the exceptions to it.[36] In any event and as a bare minimum, the national legal orders should provide for effective remedies of one sort or another as regards breaches of the obligation to refer insofar as the fundamental right to an effective judicial protection granted by the Charter is concerned.

In that context, a national court hearing a case about Article 47 of the Charter in the last instance would be bound to make a reference, as it would be adjudicating a fundamental rights claim based on Union law. In such a way, Union rights, including the right to an effective judicial protection, would be effectively safeguarded at state level. If the national remedy were to prove insufficient in a given case, the individual could seek the protection of the European Convention on Human Rights before the Strasbourg Court. The Court of Justice could also intervene in that context, once the Union accedes to the Convention, through the prior involvement procedure.

Be it before national courts or before the Strasbourg Court, the criteria used to examine whether the absence of a preliminary reference by a court adjudicating in the last instance constitutes a breach of the applicable fundamental right should not be different from those of the obligation to refer, since the right is automatically infringed when the obligation is breached. At present those criteria are laid down in the *CILFIT* case law, whose rigidity might need to be reconsidered by the Court.

This understanding of the relationship between the preliminary reference system and the fundamental right to an effective judicial protection would go a long way in enhancing the

[36] The issue of the respective scopes of national and Union fundamental rights will be addressed in chapter 6.

effectiveness and the integrity of Union law. A more rigorous practice of the preliminary rulings procedure on the part of the Court, fully exploiting its normative potential by determining with more precision the Union law issues referred to it, would also be required by the fundamental right to an effective judicial protection and by the general principle of legal certainty.

A stricter observance of the obligation to refer addressed to national courts of last resort could admittedly flood the Court with references in the same way as a European appeal could flood it with appeals. Such a flood would nonetheless be preferable to the current suboptimal situation. If the flood became real, practical solutions such as the ones evoked earlier should be sought. These difficulties, related to the organization of the administration of justice, should not stand in the way of seeking to improve the practice of the supranational rule of law in the Union.

5

PARTIAL ECLIPSE OF UNION CITIZENSHIP: FROM *GRZELCZYK* TO *DANO*

1

Union citizenship seems the obvious choice when looking for a substantive area in which to test the state of health of the law of integration, as it is paradigmatic and reflects the wider processes of decay and resistance that the Union is going through.

The topic is not easy. Legal issues surrounding citizenship are loaded with ideology, complex feelings, and irrational instincts. So much so that sometimes the conditions in which a meaningful discussion could take place do not seem to exist, even among otherwise perfectly reasonable persons. This may be due to the fact that, besides being a technical concept embodying the legal status of the members of a political community, citizenship has a broader symbolic dimension. Citizenship tends to define an identity, a difference between 'us' and 'them', and issues of identity are very difficult to analyse objectively, since the observer's own position is often at stake, preventing a neutral view on the matter.

Framing the powers of the Member States of the Union as regards the treatment of persons coming from other Member States has always been at the heart of the integration project, and remains an essential element of Union law. Beyond its socio-economic, legal, and political aspects, integration was and remains a moral endeavour. Its law cannot be properly understood if it is approached from a purely technical perspective.

The moral dimension of integration is visible in the founding texts of the 1950s, when Europe was just emerging from a long dark period in which the humanity of the other, and in particular of certain groups, was often not recognized, leading to an outright denial of their legal status, inhuman treatment, and ultimately genocide. It is also important to remember that all this was

What's Left of the Law of Integration? Decay and Resistance in European Union Law. First Edition. Julio Baquero Cruz. © Julio Baquero Cruz 2018. Published 2018 by Oxford University Press.

done with the support of state law and state jurists and officials. It was, at least in part, a bureaucratic and legal enterprise. The new European order, with its national and supranational institutions and rules, was not only meant to contribute to the aim of making war impossible, but also to overcome the inhuman treatment of the other.

The civilizational and moral aim of the European project is at the centre of the Schuman declaration, the founding constitutional document of integration. I have already referred to the institutional and legal hints contained in the declaration, but Schuman had something to say about substance as well. Although the central initial aim of the project was economic and institutional, the declaration contained various references to other objectives, such as the idea of creating 'a wider and deeper *community between peoples* long opposed to one another by sanguinary divisions'. Besides, Schuman was not silent about fundamental social aims. He proposed that the High Authority would be in charge 'of securing in the shorter possible time ... *the equalisation and improvement of the living conditions of workers in these countries*'. And he also included a reference, repeated in the preamble of the Treaty of Paris, to the establishment of a '*solidarité de fait*' among the states participating in integration.[1]

The idea of 'a wider and deeper community between peoples' entailed a recognition of those peoples as equal parts of an integrated whole. The reference to the 'equalisation and improvement of the living conditions of workers' went beyond purely formal equality, alluding to progressive substantive equality between the workers of all the Member States. Even though the initial plan was limited to one particular sector, deeper ideas of community and equality were present in it, confirming its political ambition.

Following the Schuman declaration, the Treaties did not just aim to limit and frame state sovereignty through effective and autonomous legal and institutional structures. Primary law was never an empty shell to be filled in through acts of secondary law. From the beginning, the Treaties contained significant substantive provisions.

[1] Schuman declaration, see chapter 2, note 4 (emphasis added).

The Treaty establishing the European Coal and Steel Community prohibited any form of economic discrimination among producers, buyers, or users of coal and steel products. The Member States were also bound to prohibit any discrimination in pay and working conditions between national and immigrant workers. In addition, it was established that national social security provisions should not constitute an obstacle to the movement of workers.

This incipient reflection of social principles unfolded in the Treaty of Rome, whose preamble referred to the aim of ensuring 'the economic and social progress of their countries by common action to eliminate the barriers which divide Europe', and 'by reducing the differences existing between the various regions and the backwardness of the less favoured regions'. Its Article 7 enshrined what remains today the basic substantive rule of the law of integration: 'Within the scope of application of this Treaty, and without prejudice to any special provisions contained therein, any discrimination on grounds of nationality shall be prohibited'.

The idea of non-discrimination on grounds of nationality is intrinsic to the idea of an integrated space and reaches into the realms of constitutional law and social policy. At its base, the prohibition of discrimination on grounds of nationality has to do with the protection of human dignity, which can be seen as the 'ultimate aim of the integration process'.[2] Article 7 of the Treaty of Rome (now Article 18 TFEU) reflects a fundamental moral norm: to treat the other as oneself and, beyond that, to transcend the distinction between oneself and the other. In spite of this clear command, this provision was subject to various interpretative tensions from the start, in view of the limited scope of application of the Treaty, which only covered economic activities, and of the tension between a formal and a substantive understanding of equality.

Besides the basic prohibition of discrimination, other provisions fleshed out the European solidarity and the gradual equalization and improvement of the living conditions among workers

[2] E. O. Eriksen, *The Normativity of the European Union* (2014) 106.

to which the Schuman declaration referred. Article 48(2) of the Treaty of Rome established that the free movement of workers entailed the abolition of any discrimination based on nationality between workers of the Member States, with regard to employment, pay, and other working conditions. Article 119 laid down the principle of equal pay for equal work between men and women. The prohibition of discrimination on grounds of nationality was further specified in the other economic provisions of the Treaty.

In the wake of these provisions, the Court put the status of the other at the heart of its case law from the beginning, most notably in *Van Gend en Loos*, with its conception of Community law as a new legal order which gives rights to individuals and imposes obligations on them.[3] In its free movement case law, the Court also made sure that the Treaty rules were duly respected by the states, granting them direct effect and ensuring that the rights of traders, consumers, producers, companies, workers, service providers, and service recipients were respected. The most relevant case law in this regard is that concerning the free movement of workers and gender equality. The Court has recognized that these provisions have two purposes, one economic and another social, which need to be carefully balanced in their interpretation and application.[4] In addition, in the case of workers and gender equality the principle of non-discrimination binds not only the states but also private employers, even with regard to individual contracts or unilateral offers of employment.[5]

The objection could be raised that in the initial design of integration the other was not protected in his or her own right. Besides the lower protection afforded to third-country nationals, nationals of the Member States were only considered as a means to pursue further political and economic ends, such as

[3] *Van Gend en Loos*, see chapter 2, note 7, at 12.

[4] *Defrenne*, see chapter 2, note 9, at para; 10; and Case C-341/05, *Laval*, EU:C:2007:809, at para. 105.

[5] *Defrenne*, see chapter 2, note 9; and Case C-281/98, *Angonese*, EU:C:2000:296.

the reorganization of inter-state relations in a binding framework or the increased efficiency of markets through a better allocation of the factors of production.

The economic rationale justifying the protection of workers is obvious. If all workers from all Member States are treated in accordance with the working and social conditions of the host Member State, and in the absence of natural barriers to movement (which are, however, conspicuous in the Union), labour will normally go to the country in which it is most effective for the economic process. This will lead to specialization, higher productivity, and a *net* improvement in living conditions throughout the internal market. This does not mean that all Member States will profit from integration, and indeed some may suffer from it. Besides, since workers from other Member States contribute to the welfare regime of the host country in the same terms as national workers, their equal treatment simply ensures that the Member States do not engage in unfair competition or social dumping by discriminating against workers from other Member States.

This is connected to the limited substantive scope of the Treaty of Rome. One of the conditions for the application of the original free movement rules was the existence of an economic activity, i.e. of offering or receiving goods or services in the market. In the absence of such an activity, the situation would fall outside the scope of Community law. In consequence, most situations concerning persons not engaged in the economic process, such as students, retired persons, the unemployed or the destitute, were not covered by the law of integration. Although the Court reduced that gap in some ways, affording some protection to students and service recipients, there remained a residuary category of persons left unprotected by the Treaty, even when they found themselves in a cross-border situation that would normally trigger the application of the prohibition of discrimination on grounds of nationality.

One could conclude that in the initial design of integration a natural person was never treated as a fully-fledged *civis*, with all the dimensions of citizenship (civil, political, economic, and social), but only as *homo œconomicus*, insofar as he or she engaged in economic activity—with the potential alienation implicit in this perspective.[6]

This criticism has merit, but one should not belittle the value of protecting persons from other Member States within the scope of economic activities. We spend much of our lives engaged in those activities, which are an integral part of human experience and of what it means to be a free citizen. The protection of nationals from other Member States as economic actors is not comprehensive, but it is not trite as a legal asset when one compares it with the absence of protection. Besides, the fact that there is an economic rationale for these rules does not mean that other objectives are inconceivable. While fostering economic rationality and market integration, some of the free movement rules and the basic rule of non-discrimination on the basis of nationality clearly pursue an objective of equality and fairness.

From this point of view, those rules also mean that the economic advantages which the states receive from an integrated market cannot be dissociated from an idea of fairness in that market. In other words, those benefits will necessarily come together with some burdens that they must accept as part of what it means to be a Member State of the European Union. The inextricable link between advantages and burdens or shared responsibility is one of the elements fleshing out the original objectives of establishing solidarity between the Member States, and of gradually equalizing and improving the living conditions among their workers.

2

The residuary category of economically inactive persons began to receive attention and protection from the Community with the adoption and implementation of three directives in the early 1990s.[7] These Directives went beyond the economic sphere and

[6] See M. Everson, 'The Legacy of the Market Citizen', in J. Shaw and G. More (eds.), *New Legal Dynamics of European Union* (1995) 73.

[7] Council Directive 90/364 on the right of residence; Council Directive 90/365 on the right of residence for employees and self-employed persons who have ceased their occupational activity; and Council Directive 90/366 on the

gave rights to those persons when they found themselves in cross-border situations. However, those rights were granted through instruments of secondary law and seemed modest in their ambition. In a way, the Directives protected those persons while also protecting the Member States. Inter-state solidarity seemed to be excluded in view of the requirements of sufficient economic resources and health insurance. These conditions could mean that economically inactive persons were only admitted as consumers, to spend in the market of the host state. In principle they should not represent any burden for that state.

In 1993 the Maastricht Treaty enshrined European citizenship in primary law as part of the constitutional compromise sketched in it: a complex pact between prosperous and less prosperous countries, north and south, centre and periphery, old countries and newcomers, big and small states, conservative and progressive political forces, and different views about the future of integration. Union citizenship and some other elements of the Treaty of Maastricht can be seen as the counterpart of the liberal economic logic followed by the provisions on economic and monetary union.

This balance between competing visions and values is currently reflected in Article 3(3) TEU, according to which the Union shall work not only for 'the sustainable development of a Europe based on balanced economic growth and price stability', but also for 'a highly competitive social market economy, aiming at full employment and social progress'. While it could be questioned whether this balance is sufficiently reflected in the substantive rules and policies of the Union, it is clear that the rules on Union citizenship are connected to the second part of the equation and stand in an intriguing tension with the aims of economic integration.

Following the spirit of the Schuman declaration, the Maastricht Treaty confirmed that integration was not merely about economic rationality or about profiting from access to the internal market without any attendant burden. The Treaty

right of residence for students, OJ 1990 L 180/26. After its annulment by the Court of Justice, the latter was replaced by Council Directive 93/96, OJ 1993 L 317/59.

confirmed that integration was more than an economic idea. This was reflected in the deletion of the word 'economic' from its title, a significant change justified by the addition of the rules on European citizenship and of other Treaty provisions. The progressive equalization of the conditions of living in the Member States, and an ideal of justice among those states and their peoples, remained at the heart of the European project as an indispensable complement to the economic dimension of integration.

At the time of their adoption it was argued that the provisions on Union citizenship did not have any added value, since most of the rights they contained had already been granted by the Directives mentioned earlier.[8] This criticism overlooked the crucial significance of the introduction of European citizenship in primary law. First, since the most important new provisions followed the structure of the free movement rules, they could immediately benefit from a rich case law and from its grid of analysis and adjudication technique. Secondly, the new provisions aimed to protect non-economically active persons for their own sake and not as part of the economic process, filling a gap in the system of the free movement rules which could be significant for the other rules. Finally, the rights were granted at the level of primary law, with important interpretative consequences.

The concrete impact of the new rights of free movement, residence, and non-discrimination granted to Union citizens as citizens and not only as economically active persons would depend on legislative implementation and also on judicial interpretation, with their usual interplay. But the new rules clearly pointed to the moral dimension of integration, since they had to do with the fair and equal treatment of the 'other'.

This moral dimension is even more crucial when human dignity is at stake. The issue becomes very concrete when economically inactive Union citizens from other Member States wish to benefit, pursuant to Treaty and/or legislative provisions on non-discrimination, from national benefits aimed at preserving

[8] See Weiler, chapter 2, note 17, at 326.

that dignity. Unlike the equal treatment offered to workers, this would entail a genuine form of solidarity, as those citizens may be persons who do not contribute to the society of the host state. They may be 'bad citizens', like the poor, the sick, the beggar or the vagabond, and not the 'good citizens' that all Member States would welcome with open arms.

When Union citizens in need are involved, the universal notion of human dignity clashes with the closed character of national welfare systems, which in principle protect the circle of persons who are entitled to claim solidarity rights from the relevant community. In between we find the mediating notion of European citizenship, the principle of non-discrimination attached to it, and the notion of inter-state solidarity.

3

The first important decision of the Court on Union citizenship is the judgment in *Grzelczyk*.[9] Rudy Grzelczyk, a French national, moved from France to Belgium to study physical education in 1995. In the final year of his studies he applied for the *minimex*, a Belgian subsidy for those lacking sufficient resources. His request was rejected because he did not comply with the applicable national rules, according to which the benefit was granted to all Belgians if they were majors, resided in Belgian territory and lacked adequate resources, while nationals of other Member States had to comply with an additional requirement: falling within the scope of the Regulation on the free movement of workers.[10] Mr Grzelczyk appealed and the Labour Tribunal of Nivelles sent a preliminary reference to the Court of Justice, asking whether the rules on Union citizenship precluded the application of that additional requirement, in view of its discriminatory character.

To understand the significance of the Court's judgment, it is useful to recall the opposition of some Member States to a constructive reading of the new provisions on Union citizenship.

[9] Case C-184/99, *Grzelczyk*, EU:C:2001:458.
[10] Council Regulation 1612/68, OJ 1968 L 257/2.

For the competent administrative authority of the Belgian state, the applicable Treaty provision lacked direct effect and its implementation was freely defined by secondary law, which required sufficient resources and social security cover.[11] Echoing the academic belittling of the new rules, the Belgian and Danish governments claimed that '[c]itizenship of the Union does not mean that Union citizens obtain rights that are new or more extensive than those already deriving from the EC Treaty and secondary legislation'. They argued that the principle of Union citizenship has 'no autonomous content, but is merely linked to other provisions of the Treaty'.[12] Referring to *Martínez Sala*,[13] the United Kingdom considered that the discrimination suffered by Mr Grzelczyk fell outside the personal scope of the Treaty, as he was not a worker.[14] The Commission seemed to be stuck in the interpretative dead end of *Martínez Sala* and argued that the new Treaty rules only 'operated within the scope of the application *ratione materiae* of the Treaty, provided that the Union citizen's situation has some relevant connection with the Member State concerned'.[15]

These arguments forced the Court to clarify whether the introduction of Union citizenship in the Treaty made any difference with regard to the previous legal situation, or whether the new provisions were destined to become empty rhetoric. This was linked to the more technical question of determining whether those provisions could define their own material and personal scopes of application, instead of applying only in situations which already fell within the scope of the pre-existing freedoms and legislation. If the new provisions were to have a substance of their own, the Court would also need to determine their concrete consequences for national authorities and for the Union legislature.

The first step in the Court's reasoning was to recall that this was a case of direct discrimination on grounds of nationality.[16] The application of Mr Grzelczyk was rejected *only* because he

[11] *Grzelczyk*, *supra* note 9, at para. 20.
[12] *Ibid.*, at para. 21.
[13] Case C-85/96, *Martínez Sala*, EU:C:1998:217.
[14] *Grzelczyk*, *supra* note 9, at para 24.
[15] *Ibid.*, at para. 26.
[16] *Ibid.*, at para. 29.

was a national from another Member State. This statement could seem trite but it confirms that, as with the other free movement rules, classifications based on nationality are highly suspect. More importantly, it means that nationals and non-nationals are in a comparable situation with regard to social assistance, even though it is financed through the national budget. For the Court, the relevant category was 'Union citizens', who in principle deserve equal treatment within the sphere of application of the Treaty.

The second step of the judgment was to define the scope within which the prohibition of discrimination deploys its effects. The Court rectified the preliminary position taken in *Martínez Sala*,[17] which had threatened to clip the wings of Union citizenship by linking its scope of application to the scopes of other primary or secondary law rules. In *Grzelczyk*, the Court declared that 'Article 6 must be read in conjunction with the provisions of the Treaty concerning citizenship of the Union in order to determine its sphere of application'.[18] As a result, situations involving the exercise of the right of Union citizens to move to another Member State and to reside there were within the scope of Union law,[19] regardless of whether or not those situations were covered by the substantive scope of application of other provisions of that legal order.

This passage is the 'declaration of independence' of the rules on Union citizenship. The relevant Treaty provisions autonomously determine their own scope of application, which is different from the scopes of other rules, including those on the free movement of workers. Once a European citizen moves to another Member State, his or her situation immediately falls within the scope of the Treaty, which will protect that person against discrimination—without prejudice to its possible objective justification. In practice, this means that in relation to Union citizens the substantive scope of the prohibition of discrimination on grounds of nationality is unlimited. Only its personal scope is limited, as the rule does not come into play until a Union citizen is in a cross-border situation. The new

[17] *Martínez Sala*, *supra* note 13.
[18] *Grzelczyk*, *supra* note 9, at para. 30.
[19] *Ibid.*, at paras. 32 and 33.

rules changed the legal landscape, as the prohibition of discrimination on grounds of nationality could apply to non-economic situations which were not previously covered by primary law.

The Court continued its reasoning with a solemn declaration:

> Union citizenship is destined to be the fundamental status of nationals of the Member States, enabling those who find themselves in the same situation to enjoy the same treatment in law irrespective of their nationality, subject to such exceptions as are expressly provided for.[20]

The paragraph sounds pompous and is a bit exaggerated. It is excessive to say that Union citizenship is destined to be *the fundamental status* of nationals of the Member States *tout court*. Most of the time Union citizenship will be latent and not active, since persons living in their own countries are not usually entitled to protection from the applicable provisions. Citizenship of the Union only becomes important once citizens move and require protection in another Member State. In other situations, their main status is the one granted by national law—the Union status being ancillary and complementary. This was clearly expressed in the initial source of this language, the Opinion of Advocate General La Pergola in *Martínez Sala*. For Antonio La Pergola, Union citizenship 'is the fundamental status guaranteed to the citizen of every Member State *by the legal order of the Community and now the Union*'.[21] The Treaty itself would later make this quite clear by stating that Union citizenship is 'additional to and does not replace national citizenship' (Article 20(1) TFEU). The idea was also taken up in a more precise manner in the third recital of the Citizen's Rights Directive: 'Union citizenship should be the fundamental status of nationals of the Member States *when they exercise their right of free movement and residence*'.[22]

Secondly, the strong emphasis put on the right to 'enjoy *the same treatment in law* irrespective of their nationality', while being

[20] *Ibid.*, at para. 31.

[21] Opinion of 1 July 1997, Case C-85/96, *Martínez Sala*, EU:C:1997:335, at para. 18 (emphasis added).

[22] European Parliament and Council Directive 2004/38 on the right of citizens of the Union and their family members to move and reside freely within the territory of the Member States, OJ 2004 L 158/77 (emphasis added).

'subject to such exceptions as are expressly provided for', could be misleading. It sounds like a promise of almost total assimilation, unequal treatment being the exception rather than the rule. As we will soon see, the Court's judgment and later case law are very far away from that position.

In spite of these weaknesses, the declaration performs an important function. It indicates that the Court intends to be extremely vigilant when it comes to unequal treatment on grounds of nationality, closely framing the powers of the states. It also suggests that it will take the rules on Union citizenship very seriously, interpreting them in accordance with the methods it generally uses for fundamental provisions of primary law.

The final and decisive part of the judgment concerns the conditions that may be lawfully imposed on the rights of citizens to move and reside freely in the territory of the Member States.

The Court first mentioned Article 1 of Directive 93/96,[23] which allowed the states to make the right of residence of students conditional upon three requirements: having sufficient resources, being enrolled in studies, and being covered by sickness insurance.[24] As regards sufficient resources, the Court recalled that Article 3 of the Directive did not require any specific amount or proof: a mere declaration sufficed.

The Court then noted that the states are not prevented from 'taking the view that a student who has recourse to social assistance no longer fulfils the conditions of his right of residence or from taking measures, within the limits imposed by Community law, either to withdraw his residence permit or not to renew it'. It added, nevertheless, that 'in no case may such measures become the automatic consequence of a student who is a national of another Member State having recourse to the host Member State's social assistance system'.[25]

There is a productive tension between these two statements. Once a student has recourse to social assistance, it seems fair to deduce that he or she no longer has sufficient resources and that the Member States would be entitled to withdraw the student's residence permit. For the Court such a deduction should not be

[23] Directive 93/96, *supra* note 7.

[24] *Grzelczyk*, *supra* note 9, at para. 38.

[25] *Ibid.*, at paras. 42 and 43.

automatic, however, since the preamble to the Directive states that the requirement of sufficient resources aims at avoiding that students from other states become 'an unreasonable burden' on the public finances of the host state. This meant that the states are bound to bear certain burdens, as long as they remain 'reasonable', and that the Students Directive, in the same way as the other two Directives, 'accepts *a certain degree of financial solidarity between nationals of a host Member State and nationals of other Member States*, particularly if the difficulties which a beneficiary of the right of residence encounters are *temporary*'.[26]

The most important aspect of the *Grzelczyk* judgment is its search for a balance between the prohibition of discrimination and the protection of national welfare systems. While taking non-discrimination as its point of departure, the Court does not ignore that those systems are territorial and that requiring complete equality among European citizens could seriously undermine them. What the Treaty requires is a limited measure of equality and solidarity, not complete assimilation. While reasonable burdens must be accepted, unreasonable burdens would justify discontinuing the right of residence.

This means that the Treaty does not require as much equality as could be required by national law between national citizens or by Union law itself as regards workers. The Court admits that economically inactive nationals of the host state and economically inactive nationals of other Member States may be treated differently at some point in time—but not immediately nor automatically. That is the point where a Union citizen from another state will become an unreasonable burden and where equality and cross-border solidarity would break—while solidarity could continue among nationals of the host state.

The Court's approach is neutral, fair and balanced. It does not favour emigration or immigration countries and their peoples. It tries to define Union citizenship as a legal status between full assimilation to national citizenship and the unlimited acceptance of discrimination against economically inactive European citizens, which would deprive the Treaty rules of any added value.

[26] *Ibid.*, at para. 44 (emphasis added).

As with the case law on the rights of patients in cross-border situations, which belongs to the same period,[27] the Court is trying to create limited bridges between closed systems in order to protect the situation of European citizens, framing state power while preserving the integrity of national welfare systems.

Like most productive judgments, *Grzelczyk* leads to new questions. What are the precise limits to the rights of residence of Union citizens? Where are the bounds of that 'certain degree of solidarity'? For how long will Mr Grzelczyk and other Union citizens in a similar situation be able to remain in the host state, benefiting from social assistance? When exactly will they become an 'unreasonable burden'?

While the judgment makes clear that the applicant is entitled to receive the *minimex*, the Court does not take a position on the point in time at which that 'certain degree of financial solidarity' would no longer be required, so that Mr Grzelczyk would lose his right of residence and the *minimex*. This is a consequence of the limits of the Court's role. The Court may only rule on the lawfulness of the measures adopted by the competent authorities: it is not entitled to adopt those measures. The judgment opens a process of trial and error through which those authorities will strive to find a balance that can be accepted by the Court.

Beyond its technical dimensions, this judgment tells us something important about the meaning of Union citizenship. There is an interesting symbolism in the fact that *Grzelczyk,* the Polish family name of a French student living in Belgium, which many Europeans cannot write and pronounce correctly, stands for the first leading decision on European citizenship. Perhaps the situation of that student is not only a real one but also a metaphor of what it sometimes means to be a European citizen: to be displaced and in need. From this perspective, what *Grzelczyk* offers is a moral vision of the applicable rules: the recognition of the other as not different from oneself, as deserving to be treated with human dignity, as an end instead of as an instrument of further economic ends, and the duty to ensure a measure of equality and solidarity between Union citizens.

[27] For example, Case C-157/99, *Smits and Peerbooms*, EU:C:2001:404.

4

About a year later the Court rendered its judgment in *Baumbast*, confirming, against the opposition of certain legal actors, some of the points which were implicit in *Grzelczyk*. The governments of the United Kingdom and Germany, and also the Commission, argued against the direct effect and added value of the provisions on Union citizenship, and in favour of a demotion of those rules to a rhetorical position. For those two Member States, the 'limitations and conditions' to which the provision is subject 'show that it is not intended to be a free-standing provision'.[28] The Commission also saw the provision as 'conditioned by the pre-existing rules, both primary and secondary'. The rights it granted were 'still linked either to an economic activity or to sufficient resources'. The conclusion was that, '[s]ince the point of departure for the third question is that Mr Baumbast has no other Community law foundations for his right to reside in the United Kingdom, . . . Article 18 EC cannot, as the law stands at present and in such circumstances, be of any use to him'.[29]

The judgment of the Court rejected these restrictive views. It first recalled the added value of the provisions on Union citizenship:

> Although, before the [TEU] entered into force, the Court had held that the right of residence, conferred directly by the EC Treaty, was subject to the condition that the person concerned was carrying on an economic activity . . . , it is none the less the case that, since then, Union citizenship has been introduced into the EC Treaty and Article 18(1) EC has conferred a right, for every citizen, to move and reside freely within the territory of the Member States.[30]

Secondly, it recognized direct effect. The decisive argument was that 'the application of the limitations and conditions acknowledged in Article 18(1) EC in respect of the exercise of that right of residence is subject to judicial review'. In consequence, 'any limitations and conditions imposed on that right do not prevent

[28] Case C-413/99, *Baumbast*, EU:C:2002:493, at para. 78.
[29] *Ibid.*, at para. 79. [30] *Ibid.*, at para. 81.

the provisions of Article 18(1) EC from conferring on individuals rights which are enforceable by them and which the national courts must protect'.[31] Finally, for the Court the limitations and conditions imposed by the states on the rights of Union citizens 'must be applied in compliance with the limits imposed by Community law and in accordance with the general principles of that law, in particular the principle of proportionality. That means that national measures adopted on that subject must be necessary and appropriate to attain the objective pursued.'[32] The restriction in the case in hand turned out to be a disproportionate interference with the exercise of that right.[33]

All these points are explicitly or implicitly contained in *Grzelczyk*.

First, the Court confirms that those provisions change things and that their impact will not be denied through interpretation. They do not simply reflect the previous legal situation but are of immediate use for European citizens.

Secondly, the new provisions define their own scope of application, and they do so through their personal scope, not through their substantive scope—which is no longer relevant. As soon as citizens are in a cross-border situation, they fall within the scope of the provision on Union citizenship, regardless of whether the situation is within the substantive scope of other provisions of primary or secondary Union law.[34]

Thirdly, the rules on Union citizenship, like the other free movement rules, are directly effective. Direct effect was implicit in *Grzelczyk*, which only made sense if the provisions had that effect. By answering the preliminary questions, the Court accepted that those provisions could be invoked before national courts and should be applied by the latter. In consequence, Union citizens whose situation is not linked to an economic

[31] *Ibid.*, at para. 86, referring to Case 41/74, *Van Duyn*, EU:C:1974:133, at para. 7.

[32] *Baumbast*, *supra* note 28, at para. 91.

[33] *Ibid.*, at para. 93.

[34] The autonomous scope of the new rules was reiterated in Case C-456/02, *Trojani*, EU:C:2004:488, at para. 31; and Case C-209/03, *Bidar*, EU:C:2005:169, at para. 33.

activity obtain rights on the basis of the Treaty, and not only through secondary law.

Finally, the idea that the limitations and conditions imposed by the Union legislature or by national authorities must be justified and proportionate in order to be compatible with the Treaty was also implicit in *Grzelczyk*. The need to accept a burden as long as it is 'reasonable' reflected the principle of proportionality. Refusing to bear reasonable burdens could render disproportionate and unlawful the limitations imposed by Union legislation or by national measures. The judgment in *Baumbast* confirms that the rules on Union citizenship not only frame and limit state power; they also bind the political institutions of the Union and entail limits for the secondary law that they may adopt, limits that may be reviewed by the Court in the light of the principle of proportionality.

Not long after *Baumbast*, in *Collins*, a case concerning a jobseeker's allowance, the Court admitted that it was legitimate for a Member State to ensure that there is 'a *genuine link* between an applicant for an allowance in the nature of a social advantage within the meaning of Article 7(2) of Regulation No 1612/68 and the geographic employment market in question'. Lawful residence of a certain length could be required to establish such a link, but the length had to be proportionate. While leaving the concrete decision to the referring court, the Court suggested that a fairly short stay would be sufficient, as a genuine link could be established if 'the person concerned has, for a reasonable period, in fact genuinely sought work in the Member State in question'.[35]

The requirement of a 'genuine link' with the host state would have a remarkable career, developing in unexpected ways. For the time being, however, it was just a reasonable reflection of the bounds of supranational solidarity, reflecting the basic ideas of 'a certain degree of solidarity' and 'reasonable burden', preventing opportunistic behaviour, and protecting the sustainability of national welfare systems. Besides, that requirement only

[35] Case C-138/02, *Collins*, EU:C:2004:172, at para. 69–73 (emphasis added). The notion of a 'real link' had been used in Case C-224/98, *D'Hoop*, EU: C:2002:432, at para. 38. Regulation 1612/68 is referred to *supra* note 10.

seemed to apply to social advantages and not to social assistance aimed at safeguarding basic human dignity—which could not depend on such a link. Moreover, the Court was strict in its proportionality review, suggesting that national measures that made social advantages dependent on very long periods of residence would be in breach of Union law.

Trojani is the next important episode in the 'chain novel' of the case law on Union citizenship, for one main reason. The case is very similar to *Grzelczyk*, as it also concerns the Belgian *minimex*, and most of the judgment simply refers to that precedent. But there is a significant difference, as Mr Trojani was not a student: he was a homeless person who had lacked sufficient resources to live on from the beginning of his stay in Belgium. In consequence, Union law did not grant him a right of residence. For the Court, 'there is no indication that, in a situation such as that at issue in the main proceedings, the failure to recognise that right would go beyond what is necessary to achieve the objective pursued by that directive'.[36] Nevertheless, the judgment recalled that Mr Trojani 'is lawfully resident in Belgium, as is attested by the residence permit which has in the meantime been issued to him by the municipal authorities of Brussels'. This lawful residence, granted as a matter of national law, entails the applicability of the Treaty provision on non-discrimination on grounds of nationality.[37] Union citizens who are lawfully resident in a Member State may therefore invoke the prohibition of discrimination on grounds of nationality, even when their right of residence results from national law and not from Union law.

The next significant step in the development of the case law on Union citizenship is the judgment in *Chen*. Mrs Chen took up residence in Ireland 'in order to enable the child she was expecting to acquire Irish nationality and, consequently, to enable her to acquire the right to reside, should the occasion arise, with her child in the United Kingdom'.[38] Since her application for a long-term permit to reside in the United Kingdom was rejected by the British authorities, she sought the protection of the Treaty rules on Union citizenship, and

[36] *Trojani*, *supra* note 34, at paras. 36–9. [37] *Ibid.*, at para. 37.
[38] Case C-200/02, Chen, EU:C:2004:639, at para. 11.

the Immigration Appellate Authority of the United Kingdom sent a preliminary reference to the Court of Justice.

The main point in *Chen* was about the issue of abuse of law. The British authorities argued that Mrs Chen had moved to Ireland in order for her child to acquire Irish nationality and be entitled to reside with her in the United Kingdom. For that Member State, this would have been 'an attempt improperly to exploit the provisions of Community law'.[39] The Court rejected this claim. Although the purpose of Mrs Chen's stay was to secure for her child and for herself a long-term right of residence in the United Kingdom, this was the mere effect of the applicable nationality rules.[40] Although the Court did not refer to it, this approach is inspired by the case law regarding the economic freedoms, according to which the mere exercise of a free movement right can never amount to an abuse of rights, because benefiting from the possibilities opened by the single market is 'inherent in the exercise' of those freedoms.[41]

The next significant episode, the judgment of 15 March 2005 in *Bidar*, marks the end of the ascending line of the Court's citizenship case law. From then onwards, with a few exceptions, the Court of Justice would be much more sensitive to the concerns of the Member States, adopting a rather open-handed approach to the issue of what they are entitled to require to establish a 'genuine link', while trying to preserve a minimum of effectiveness for the provisions on Union citizenship.

The efforts of the Court to preserve a degree of effectiveness are visible in its confirmation of the autonomous scope and added value of the Treaty rules on citizenship. Although secondary law excluded the right to maintenance assistance for students, the Court held that that right could be based directly on the fundamental principle of equal treatment enshrined in the Treaty.[42] In line with *Trojani*, the Treaty rules on citizenship are not only independent from other Union rules, having direct effect and determining the legality of secondary and national

[39] *Ibid.*, at para. 34.
[40] *Ibid.*, at paras. 36–41.
[41] Case C-212/97, *Centros*, EU:C:1999:126, at para. 27.
[42] *Bidar*, *supra* note 34, at paras. 45 and 46.

law: they may go beyond Union legislation and confer rights which that legislation does not grant.

Bidar also repeats previous case law when it requires a 'certain degree of financial solidarity with nationals of other Member States', which involves bearing reasonable burdens. At the same time, the Court accepts that maintenance assistance may only be granted to students from other Member States 'who have demonstrated *a certain degree of integration* into the society of that State'. For the Court, the states cannot require a link with the employment market, but only to have 'resided in the host Member State for a certain length of time'. The judgment is however rather lenient with the host Member State, as it implicitly accepts that a three years' residence requirement, met by Mr Bidar, is reasonable.[43] The applicable national rules also required the applicant to be considered as 'settled', a condition that was very difficult to fulfil by nationals of other Member States. This treatment was not justified, as it would prevent a student who had a 'genuine link' with the United Kingdom, in view of his long residence there, from receiving equal treatment.

In a further *diminuendo*, the *Förster* judgment[44] found that the five years' residence requirement imposed by Germany to establish a genuine link and have access to student maintenance grants was acceptable. Significantly, the judgment based its analysis of primary law (by analogy) on Article 24(2) of Directive 2004/38 on the rights of citizens,[45] which, though not applicable to the case in hand, allowed the Member States to require a five-year lawful residence to have a right to maintenance grants for studies.

Directive 2004/38, an important piece in the development of the law on Union citizenship, was meant to increase legal certainty, defining the extent of the right to equal treatment and the bounds of supranational solidarity. The Directive took the case law into account, in particular the judgment in *Grzelczyk*, whose language it echoed several times. However, this piece of secondary law was not a mere codification of the case law.

[43] *Ibid.*, at paras. 56–61.

[44] Case C-158/07, *Förster*, EU:C:2008:630, at paras. 51–8.

[45] Directive 2004/38, *supra* note 22.

Throughout its provisions it is possible to see the tension between the need to assess the concrete situation of each Union citizen in the light of the principle of proportionality, as required by the case law, and the wish to establish, through clear time periods, a simpler system for the Member States. Thus, for Union citizens who are lawfully resident for less than three months, the Directive grants an unconditional right of residence but rules out access to any social benefits, including social assistance. At the same time, Directive 2004/38 establishes a relation between expulsion and a request of social assistance, but it excludes any automaticity in full respect of *Grzelczyk*. Between three months and five years, a conditional right of residence is granted to non-workers, but some benefits remain excluded. After five years of lawful residence, Union citizens acquire a permanent right of residence and full equality regarding social benefits. All those limits to equal treatment are however expressly declared to be 'subject to the Treaty' (Article 24 of Directive 2004/38). The possibility of obtaining more rights as a matter of primary law is thus reserved. It seems clear that the Union legislature did not want to (and indeed could not) exhaust primary law or to meddle with it.

This unstable state of affairs, reflecting a precarious balance between equality and the protection of welfare systems, between primary and secondary law, and between individual assessments and clear-cut rules, characterized the period following the implementation of Directive 2004/38. It is difficult to assess how far these jurisprudential and legislative rules were reflected in the administrative practices of the Member States. Preliminary references have been relatively abundant in this field, but are they the emerging part of an iceberg of compliance or of benign neglect of the requirements of Union law? We do not know whether the treatment of economically inactive citizens in the Member States actually corresponded to what Directive 2004/38 and the case law based on the Treaty required.

The rigid approach followed by the Directive may be problematic from the perspective of the primary law rules on Union citizenship. When discussing *Collins*, I suggested that the requirement of a 'genuine link' with the host state, to be established through a period of residence and strictly framed by the Court in terms of proportionality, reflected the idea of a 'reasonable burden', aiming to protect national welfare systems from opportunistic behaviour while safeguarding the rights of Union citizens. In this respect, time is of the essence. The longer the residence requirement deemed acceptable by the Court, the weaker the solidarity between the states; the narrower the space for a 'reasonable burden', the wider the space for unequal treatment, the thinner the status of Union citizens not engaged in economic activity, and the thicker the competing notion of 'national community'.

From that perspective, one could argue that the Court's acceptance of a three-year residence requirement in *Bidar* and of a five-year requirement in *Förster*, and the legislature's acceptance of similar timeframes in Directive 2004/38, might go beyond what could reasonably be needed to achieve those legitimate objectives. It is hard to imagine that anyone would seriously consider moving to another Member State in order to apply for a maintenance grant so many years later. This very soft application of the principle of proportionality greatly reduces the 'certain degree of solidarity' to which *Grzelczyk* referred and the right of Union citizens to equality. In addition, in its deferral to the choices made by the Union legislature the Court conflates primary and secondary law, not playing its constitutional role vis-à-vis the political institutions.

Let it be clear, however, that the requirement of a 'genuine link' through prolonged residence remained confined to social advantages aimed at improving the living conditions of their recipients beyond basic human dignity, such as unemployment allowances, student subsidies, or jobseeker allowances, and was never applied to social assistance ensuring basic human dignity. Indeed, it would seem odd to accept that one needs to be lawfully resident in a Member State for, say, five years, to have a right to receive the social assistance required to preserve human dignity. From this perspective, cases concerning social advantages, such as *Collins*, *Bidar*, or *Förster* should be distinguished from cases concerning social assistance, such as *Grzelczyk* and *Trojani*. While one would need to establish a 'genuine link' before being entitled to social advantages, the case law implied that lawful residents could get social assistance from the start, without any such link, and receive it for as long as they did not become an unreasonable burden for the host state, in which case that state could lawfully withdraw the right of residence.

In parallel to the consolidation of the deferential case law on the 'genuine link', other judgments followed a more robust line. As with the economic free movement rules, a restriction-based approach was added to non-discrimination as regards the free movement of citizens.[46] What is more, in *Ruiz Zambrano*[47] the rules on Union citizenship were applied in a purely internal situation, which would generally fall outside the scope of Union law. In that case, the deportation of a married couple of third-country nationals would have forced their dependent infant children, who had Belgian nationality by birth and thus were Union citizens, to follow them and to leave the Union. For the Court this extreme interference with the citizenship rights conferred by Union law was unacceptable, even in a purely internal situation, as it had the effect of denying the very substance of those rights. Behind the idea of the 'very substance of the right', which is well known to Union law and to fundamental rights law, there is a strong moral reading of the applicable rules and an awareness of the implications for the fundamental rights of children and family life.

Soon thereafter, nevertheless, the judgment in *Ruiz Zambrano* was held to apply only in cases of dependency, in which the deportation of third-country nationals would necessarily entail the denial of the right of residence of a dependent Union citizen, and not to cases of non-dependent family members such as spouses or non-dependent children.[48] This distinction between dependent Union citizens, who receive protection from Union law even in a purely internal situation, and non-dependent Union citizens, who would only receive protection

[46] See the judgment in *D'Hoop*, *supra* note 35; Case C-224/02, *Pusa*, EU:C:2004:273; and Case C-406/04, *De Cuyper*, EU:C:2006:491.

[47] Case C-34/09, *Ruiz Zambrano*, EU:C:2011:124.

[48] Case C-434/09, *McCarthy*, EU:C:2011:277; Case C-256/11, *Dereci*, EU:C:2011:734; and Joined Cases C-356/11 and C-357/11, *O and S*, EU:C:2012:776.

in cross-border cases, leads to tragic choices. In such a case, the family is confronted with the alternative or living apart or of moving together to the third country, if that country would grant a right of residence to the Union citizens.

From a fundamental rights perspective, such a choice is hard to justify. The deciding factor in the Court's approach, which is dependency, leads to paradoxical results. It is clear that in one case there is no choice, while in the other there is a (tragic) choice. The dependent children would have to leave the Union. They cannot opt to stay, and that clearly leads to a denial of the very substance of the right. The independent close relatives, such as adult children or spouses, may decide to leave or to stay and live apart from their third-country relatives. What is difficult to understand is why that choice does not also amount to a denial of the very substance of the right, for the decision to stay would negate the fundamental right to family life, while the decision to leave would negate the rights of Union citizens. If *Ruiz Zambrano* was correctly decided, then there is no reason why Union law would not apply in a purely internal situation in which a state measure forces a Union citizen to choose between family life and Union rights.

The last important episode before *Dano* is the judgment in *Brey*, where a chamber of the Court ruled on a case about the request of a German retired person who lived in Austria and applied for Austrian social assistance. The judgment, rendered on 19 September 2013, was exclusively based on the Citizens' Rights Directive, and did not consider primary law.

Social assistance within the meaning of the Directive was held to cover '*all assistance* introduced by the public authorities, whether at national, regional or local level, *that can be claimed by an individual who does not have resources sufficient to meet his own basic needs and the needs of his family* . . .'.[49] For the Court, the fact of applying for such a benefit 'could be an indication that that national does not have sufficient resources to avoid becoming an unreasonable burden on the social assistance system of the host Member State for the purposes of Article 7(1)(b) of Directive

[49] Case C-140/12, *Brey*, EU:C:2013:565, at para. 61 (emphasis added).

2004/38'. However, the Court added, 'the competent national authorities cannot draw such conclusions without first carrying out *an overall assessment of the specific burden which granting that benefit would place on the national social assistance system as a whole, by reference to the personal circumstances characterising the individual situation of the person concerned*'.[50]

This assessment aims at locating the limits of the 'degree of financial solidarity' recognized by the Directive, following established case law based on primary law. The automaticity of the Austrian system made it incompatible with Union law, as it did not enable the competent national authorities to carry out 'an overall assessment of the specific burden which granting that benefit would place on the social assistance system as a whole by reference to the personal circumstances characterizing the individual situation of the person concerned'.[51] For the Court, those authorities should take the following elements into consideration:

> the amount and regularity of the income which he receives; the fact that those factors have led those authorities to issue him with a certificate of residence; and the period during which the benefit applied for is likely to be granted to him. In addition, in order to ascertain more precisely the extent of the burden which that grant would place on the national social assistance system, it may be relevant, as the Commission argued at the hearing, to determine the proportion of the beneficiaries of that benefit who are Union citizens in receipt of a retirement pension in another Member State.[52]

Building on the principles stated in *Grzelczyk* and codified in the Directive, *Brey* framed the powers of national administrative authorities in order to avoid arbitrary decisions and to protect the rights granted by Union law. The individual assessment required from national administrations and courts sought a reasonable balance between the rights of citizens and the legitimate interests of the Member States, barring the states from invoking those interests in the absence of a proportionate justification.

[50] *Ibid.*, at para. 64 (emphasis added).

[51] *Ibid.*, at para. 77.

[52] *Ibid.*, at para. 78.

5

The latest significant episode of this story is the judgment of the Grand Chamber of the Court of Justice of 11 November 2014, in the *Dano* case. In view of its implicit but far-reaching reversal of the previous legal position, this decision deserves detailed attention.

The facts of the main case, as reported by the Court, concerned Ms Elisabeta Dano, a young Romanian woman—and hence a citizen of the Union—born in 1989 who had lived in Germany since 2009. She had a child of unknown father, Florin Dano, also of Romanian nationality, born in Germany in July 2009. On 19 July 2011, 'the city of Leipzig issued [her] with *a residence certificate of unlimited duration*... for EU nationals, establishing 27 June 2011 as the date of entry into German territory'. The Court stated that she received a 'child benefit' for her son, amounting to 184 euros per month, and 133 euros as an advance on maintenance payments for that child. In addition, the court recalled that mother and son lived in the apartment of her sister, 'who provides for them materially', that Ms Dano knew basic oral German but had no writing skills, that she 'has not been trained in a profession and, to date, has not worked in Germany or Romania', and that '[a]lthough her ability to work is not in dispute, there is nothing to indicate that she has looked for a job'.[53]

In September 2011 and January 2012, Ms Dano and her son requested a 'subsistence benefit' which is, according to the German Social Code, 'intended to enable [their] beneficiaries to lead a life in keeping with human dignity'. Both requests were refused by the national authorities. Ms Dano and her son appealed the second decision and the Social Court of Leipzig sent a preliminary reference to the Court. The main question was whether the Treaty rules on Union citizenship and the Citizens' Rights Directive precluded the host state from excluding from social assistance nationals of other states 'who are not economically active', even though those benefits would be

[53] Case C-333/13, *Dano*, EU:C:2014:2358, at paras. 35–9 (emphasis added).

granted to nationals of the host Member State 'who are in the same situation'.[54]

The Court started its reasoning with the usual general statements, recalling that 'the status of citizen of the Union is destined to be the fundamental status of nationals of the Member States', and that Union citizens may rely on the prohibition of discrimination on grounds of nationality in situations 'relating to the exercise of the right to move and reside within the territory of the Member States'.[55] These solemn declarations, remnants of past case law, could have a melancholy or ironic tinge here, as the Court immediately set out to exclude the applicability of the prohibition of discrimination in a category of cases, changing its case law in such a way that the status of Union citizens no longer seems so fundamental.

Following the Opinion of Advocate General Wathelet,[56] the next step in the reasoning of the Court was to declare that 'the principle of non-discrimination, laid down *generally* in Article 18 TFEU, *is given more specific expression in Article 24 of Directive 2004/38* in relation to Union citizens who, like the applicants in the main proceedings, exercise their right to move and reside within the territory of the Member States'.[57] The same applied to Regulation 883/2004. For the Court, this meant that it 'should interpret Article 24 of Directive 2004/38 and Article 4 of Regulation No 883/2004'.[58]

Having narrowed down the scope of the interpretation requested by the referring court, excluding primary law, the Court repeated a key paragraph of the judgment in *Brey*.[59] This could suggest a continuity rather than a break with prior case law, leading to a balancing between equality and the coverage of basic needs,

[54] *Ibid.*, at paras. 19, 24, 40, 41, and 56 (emphasis added).

[55] *Ibid.*, at paras. 58 and 59.

[56] Opinion of 20 May 2014 (EU:C:2014:341).

[57] *Ibid.*, at points 90 and 91 (emphasis added).

[58] *Dano*, *supra* note 53, at paras. 61 and 62 (emphasis added). Directive 2004/38, *supra* note 22. European Parliament and Council Regulation No 883/2004 on the coordination of social security systems, OJ 2004 L 166/1).

[59] *Dano*, *supra* note 53, at para. 63, referring to para. 61 in *Brey*, *supra* note 49.

on the one hand, and the consequences for the overall level of assistance in the host state, on the other.

At this juncture, however, the judgment took a surprising turn. The Court recalled that Article 24(2) of the Directive established a derogation from the principle of non-discrimination during the first three months of residence. Since Ms Dano had resided in Germany for more than three months, her situation was not covered by that derogation but by Article 24(1) of the Directive.[60] The Court then noted that that provision granted a right of equal treatment to Union citizens 'residing on the basis of the directive on the territory of the host Member State', which meant that 'a Union citizen can claim equal treatment with nationals of the host Member State *only* if his residence in the territory of the host Member State complies with the conditions of Directive 2004/38'.[61] After that, the Court mentioned the three main situations traced by the Directive: residence for less than three months; between three months and five years (the situation of Ms Dano); and for more than five years.[62] And we get to the heart of the judgment.

First of all, the Court posited that:

> [i]n order to determine whether economically inactive Union citizens, [. . .] whose period of residence in the host Member State has been longer than three months but shorter than five years, can claim equal treatment with nationals of that Member State so far as concerns entitlement to social benefits, it must therefore be examined whether the residence of those citizens complies with the conditions in Article 7(1)(b) of Directive 2004/38. Those conditions include the requirement that the economically inactive Union citizen must have sufficient resources for himself and his family members.[63]

Secondly, the Court stated that:

> [t]o accept that persons who do not have a right of residence under Directive 2004/38 may claim entitlement to social benefits under the same conditions as those applicable to nationals of the host Member State *would run counter to an objective of the directive*, set out in recital 10 in its preamble, namely preventing Union citizens who are nationals of

[60] *Dano*, *supra* note 53, at paras. 64–7. [61] *Ibid.*, at paras. 68 and 69.
[62] *Ibid.*, at paras. 70–2. [63] *Ibid.*, at para. 73.

other Member States from becoming *an unreasonable burden* on the social assistance system of the host Member State.[64]

The situation of workers would be totally different from that of 'economically inactive' Union citizens. The Court thus deduced that 'Article 7(1)(b) of Directive 2004/38 seeks to prevent economically inactive Union citizens from using the host Member State's welfare system to fund their means of subsistence'.[65] In consequence:

any unequal treatment between Union citizens who have made use of their freedom of movement and residence and nationals of the host Member State with regard to the grant of social benefits is *an inevitable consequence of Directive 2004/38*. Such potential unequal treatment is founded on *the link* established by the Union legislature in Article 7 of the directive between *the requirement to have sufficient resources as a condition for residence and the concern not to create a burden on the social assistance systems of the Member States.*[66]

The conclusion could hardly be more radical:

A Member State *must therefore have the possibility*, pursuant to Article 7 of Directive 2004/38, of refusing to grant social benefits to economically inactive Union citizens who exercise their right to freedom of movement *solely in order to obtain another Member State's social assistance although they do not have sufficient resources to claim a right of residence.*[67]

For the Court:

[t]o deny the Member State concerned that possibility would . . . thus have the consequence that persons who, upon arriving in the territory of another Member State, do not have sufficient resources to provide for themselves *would have them automatically*, through the grant of a special non-contributory cash benefit which is intended to cover the beneficiary's subsistence costs.[68]

Since the applicants in the main proceedings 'do not have sufficient resources and thus cannot claim a right of residence

[64] *Ibid.*, at para. 74 (emphasis added).
[65] *Ibid.*, at para. 76 (emphasis added).
[66] *Ibid.*, at para. 77 (emphasis added).
[67] *Ibid.*, at para. 78 (emphasis added).
[68] *Ibid.*, at para. 79 (emphasis added).

in the host Member State under Directive 2004/38', 'they cannot invoke the principle of non-discrimination in Article 24(1) of the directive'. In consequence, the Directive did not preclude national legislation from excluding 'nationals of other Member States who do not have a right of residence under Directive 2004/38 in the host Member State from entitlement to certain "special non-contributory cash benefits" within the meaning of Article 70(2) of Regulation No 883/2004'.[69]

The last issue raised by the referring court, of whether economically inactive Union citizens might nonetheless obtain protection under the Charter of Fundamental Rights of the Union, was curtly evacuated at the end of the judgment: 'when the Member States lay down the conditions for the grant of special non-contributory cash benefits and the extent of such benefits, *they are not implementing EU law*'. The Court thus considered that it lacked jurisdiction to answer that question.[70]

Subsequent case law has confirmed and extended the *Dano* approach, applying it to jobseekers, to former short-time workers, and to social security benefits in the framework of the Regulation on the coordination of social security systems;[71] widening the notion of 'social assistance' to encompass some social benefits; confirming the power of the states to automatically refuse assistance for Union citizens in such situations and to use an absolute presumption of an unreasonable burden for the finances of the host state; and excluding the need for an individual assessment of the situation of those citizens and any genuine proportionality analysis.[72] The new line of case law seems so settled that the Commission has proposed codifying it in the Regulation on the coordination of social security systems.[73]

[69] *Ibid.*, at paras. 81–2.

[70] *Ibid.*, at paras. 91 and 92 (emphasis added).

[71] Regulation 883/2004, *supra* note 58.

[72] Case C-67/14, *Alimanovic*, EU:C:2015:597; Case C-299/14, *García-Nieto*, EU:C:2016:114; and Case C-308/14, *Commission v. United Kingdom*, EU:C:2016:436. See Nic Shuibhne, '"What I tell You Three Times is True": Lawful Residence and Equal Treatment after *Dano*', *Maastricht Journal of European and Comparative Law* (2016) 908.

[73] Proposal for a Regulation of the European Parliament and of the Council amending Regulation 883/2004, COM(2016) 815 final, of 13 December 2016.

6

From the perspective of legal technique, the *Dano* judgment is most perplexing.

The first perplexity is the way in which the Court disposes of the issue of Treaty interpretation, which was raised by the referring court as a distinct preliminary question. Article 18 TFEU is seen as a general proposition which is given 'more specific expression' in Union legislation. This kind of understanding of the interaction between the Treaties and secondary law is not uncommon, but it usually serves to ensure that Union legislation complies with the requirements of primary law.[74] In *Dano*, by contrast, the Treaties are eclipsed by Union legislation, which is interpreted autonomously. The compatibility of that legislation with the Treaties is taken for granted. One has the impression that the Union legislature is given an unfettered power to regulate the rights of Union citizens and to introduce blanket derogations to the fundamental rule of non-discrimination on grounds of nationality. Finally, the meaning of the Treaty does not seem to be reserved for future jurisprudential developments. What the Court does is to make it coincide with that of Article 24 of the Citizens' Rights Directive. The Court seems to be delegating the task of interpreting primary law to the Union legislature, with the practical effect of demoting Article 18 TFEU, at least for the category of persons concerned by *Dano*, to the rank of secondary law.

This is questionable for various reasons. As we have seen, the Court has recognized that the Treaty provisions on Union citizenship are directly effective and grant individual rights, protected against national measures and also against acts of the Union legislature. All limitations concerning those rights should respect the principle of proportionality. Indeed, as recalled earlier, the legislature took great care to avoid any potential breach of primary law by providing, in Article 24(1) of Citizens' Rights Directive (the provision on equal treatment), that that rule is '[s]ubject to such specific provisions as are expressly provided for in the Treaty and secondary law'. Article 24 of the Directive was

[74] See, e.g., Case C-555/07, *Kücükdeveci*, EU:C:2010:21, at para. 21.

never meant to replace the Treaty provision, and could not do so, but this seems to be ignored by the Court when it states that the right to equal treatment may *only* be invoked if the Union citizen's residence in the territory of the host state complies with the conditions of the Directive.

In contrast with the prudent approach of the legislature, *Dano* compromises the added value of the insertion of the citizenship provisions into primary law. If it were generalized, this approach would erode the judicial protection of Treaty rights and narrow down the role of the Court in the Union system. Nevertheless, *Dano* does not introduce a new paradigm for the relations between primary and secondary Union law. Its approach is only relevant for the provisions on Union citizenship *in so far as they apply to economically inactive citizens. Dano* means that in many cases the inclusion of those provisions in the Treaties will no longer have legal consequences for 'inactive' persons—i.e. for those who actually benefited from them, since workers and other economic actors were already protected by the free movement rules. The restrictive views that the Court had rejected in *Grzelczyk* and *Baumbast* seem to have been vindicated.

It is only from such a dubious premise that the Court could claim that 'any unequal treatment between Union citizens who have made use of their freedom of movement and residence and nationals of the host Member State with regard to the grant of social benefits *is an inevitable consequence of Directive 2004/38*'. If the Court had addressed the questions of the referring court concerning primary law, or if it had interpreted the Directive in the light of the Treaty, its judgment could have framed the powers of the host state and avoided any unjustified unequal treatment. There is, therefore, nothing inevitable in the inequalities resulting from its judgment.

The partial eclipse of the Treaty rules on citizenship narrows down the scope of the prohibition of discrimination on grounds of nationality. That provision will only apply, as a matter of secondary law, when a Union citizen has a right of residence *pursuant to the Directive*. For economically inactive citizens, primary law no longer defines its own scope of application. The fact that Ms Dano had a residence certificate of unlimited duration issued by the competent national authorities was ignored by the Court, in contradiction with previous judgments such as the case of Mr Trojani, who was 'lawfully resident in Belgium' as a matter of Belgian law and was protected by the Treaty. The eclipse of primary law leads to a reduction of the scope of Union law. The abandoned normative space is immediately occupied by national law.

This redefinition of the boundaries between Union law and national law is problematic. The applicability of the Treaty rules on the free movement of citizens to such situations would seem a matter of course. If a Union citizen is lawfully resident in another Member State, even if his or her residence right is granted by national law, that person is in a regular cross-border situation which should be subject to Union law. In such a case, the person should be treated in a non-discriminatory manner unless there are objective grounds justifying a different treatment. If economically inactive and lawfully resident persons in a cross-border situation are excluded from the scope of Union law, the system fails in its basic function of protecting the nationals of the Member States when they are in another Member State. The 'fundamental status' of Union citizenship is significantly eroded.

Dano not only shrinks primary law, implicitly overruling *Grzelczyk* and *Trojani*: it also rewrites part of the Citizens' Rights Directive, or at least gives a very selective reading thereof. The approach of the Directive, which codified and abundantly quoted *Grzelczyk*, was that the requirement of sufficient resources was subject to the principle of proportionality and to an individual assessment of the situation of the Union citizen. This was the bottom line of *Grzelczyk*, as reflected in the Directive and maintained all the way until *Brey*. From recital 16 and Article 8(4) of the Directive, it is clear that recourse to social assistance was not supposed to lead to the automatic expulsion of those applying for it, that no 'fixed amount' could be required as 'sufficient resources', and that the personal circumstances of Union citizens had to be assessed by the national authorities before considering that those citizens had become an unreasonable burden on the host state and proceeding to their expulsion. This was the balanced approach followed by the Court and by the Union legislature on the basis of the Treaty. It excluded automatisms and presumptions, framing the powers of the states, preventing arbitrariness, protecting the position of citizens in cross-border situations, and commanding a limited but genuine solidarity between the states. As already stated, there was no complete assimilation as the Court recognized a large space for unequal treatment, objectively justified in view of the need to protect the national welfare systems from unreasonable burdens that could endanger their sustainability. But equal treatment had to be secured as long as those burdens remained reasonable.

Not so for the *Dano* Court. The expression 'certain degree of solidarity' has disappeared from sight. The judgment excludes inactive persons from the protection previously afforded by primary and secondary Union law, introducing an automatic and absolute presumption that they represent an unreasonable burden for the host state as soon as they apply for social assistance. Any burden becomes an unreasonable burden. The choice of words is telling: for the Court, the states '*must*... have the possibility' of refusing such requests automatically. The mere fact that a person who has been resident in a Member State for more than three months and less than five years applies for social benefits is sufficient to establish an unreasonable burden for the welfare system of that state. As a result, the examination of the situation of that person is reduced to a purely formal exercise. The competent national authorities no longer need to assess whether the burden is reasonable or unreasonable. They just need to determine, without taking into account the social benefits applied for, whether that person meets the condition of having sufficient resources to qualify for a right of residence pursuant to the Directive. The circle is closed.

One passage of the *Dano* judgment seems to refer to the idea of *abuse of rights*. It allows the Member States the possibility of considering that economically inactive Union citizens who apply for social assistance have exercised their right to freedom of movement 'solely in order to obtain' that assistance, while 'they do not have sufficient resources to claim a right of residence'. One wonders how it is possible to conclude so quickly that inactive citizens who apply for social assistance between the third month and the fifth year of their residence actually moved to the host state *with the sole aim* of taking advantage of the host state's welfare system, and not for more legitimate and obvious reasons, such as looking for a better life and better professional prospects for themselves and their families. Besides, this presumption seems groundless in the case in hand. Ms Dano first moved into Germany in 2009 and only applied for the German subsidy aimed at allowing persons to live in accordance to basic human dignity in 2011. The idea that she moved to Germany in 2009 'solely in order' to apply for a social subsidy in 2011 seems rather farfetched.

A presumption of an abuse of rights or of opportunistic behaviour is in contradiction with the idea in *Chen* and in general free movement case law that the mere exercise of a right cannot constitute an abuse of that right—without prejudice to the acceptance of proportionate restrictions based on grounds of general interest.

The position taken by the Court on the scope of the Charter is equally dubious. When a Member State lays down general conditions regarding social assistance, its action is framed by Union law in so far as it concerns Union citizens from other Member States. From the perspective of primary law, those rules fall within its scope when they are to be applied to Union citizens who have exercised their free movement rights and find themselves in a cross-border situation. This means, following *Fransson*, that their situation is also within the scope of the Charter, which is coterminous with the scope of Union law.[75] We witness, once again, an *ad hoc* solution for a category of persons, the economically inactive Union citizens in cross-border situations, who have been singled out for a special legal treatment.

7

The departure of *Dano* from the standard case law on free movement and Union citizenship and its partial rewriting of secondary law are hard to justify in legal terms. There were no compelling reasons for the Court to tread down its precedents so

[75] Case C-617/10, *Åkerberg Fransson*, EU:C:2013:105. On the scope of the Charter, see chapter 6.

carelessly. The Court could have applied its settled jurisprudence, guiding the national court in the individual assessment required by the case law. This could have led, on the basis of objective data, to considering that Ms Dano already represented an unreasonable burden, or else to concluding that she had been entitled to social assistance for some time. In the second case, if after that time she had not integrated into the economic life of the host state and, following a detailed assessment of her situation, the competent national authorities found that she had become an unreasonable burden, she would lose her right of residence and would have to be returned to Romania.

The Court, however, felt bound to do something far more drastic, that cannot be reconciled with a line of case law in which it does not fit as it is an implicit but clear overruling that contradicts basic conceptions of free movement law. But this oddness wanes as soon as one sees it as a political event belonging to the complex process of bargaining around the nature of the Union and the consequences of being a Member State.

From this wider perspective, *Dano* can be seen as a reaction to the exceptional political pressure under which the Court was adjudicating. The contemporary climate of revived nationalism, disintegration, and 'Brexit' (a word that, beyond its literal meaning, seems to epitomize the current malaise in integration) was reflected in the observations lodged by prosperous countries with high levels of social protection (Germany, Denmark, Ireland, France, and the United Kingdom), while the Member States whose displaced nationals could benefit from the earlier case law remained conspicuously silent. This pressure led the Court to what could have been intended as a 'switch in time', in a particular field, in an attempt to protect its authority in other areas which it might have considered more vital for the basic structure of integration.

Perhaps the Court thought it was offering a small sacrifice of a symbolic but rather limited nature,[76] a concession devoid of major macroeconomic implications in view of the marginal

[76] The idea of 'sacrifice' has also been evoked by O'Brien, 'The ECJ Sacrifices EU Citizenship in Vain', *Common Market Law Review* (2017) 209, writing on *Commission v. United Kingdom, supra* note 72.

significance of the category of persons involved—the economically inactive in need and in a cross-border situation. At the time, the idea might have been that this could have had a positive influence on the 'Brexit' debate, by helping the case of the 'remain' camp, or that it could indirectly protect the case law on the free movement of workers, less directly related case law, or the integrity of Union law at large.

The pressure exerted on the Court was an example of the widespread utilitarian conception according to which integration is a purely economic endeavour and the Treaties are commercial agreements based on mere cooperation and entailing as little solidarity as possible. In the context of a complex, deep, and protracted economic crisis, some Member States strive to reduce the costs of integration to a minimum, while maximizing its benefits. Following that conception, the more prosperous states fear that the so-called 'benefits tourism' from nationals of other Member States could seriously harm their welfare systems. Those states claim that they should be able to control their systems and refuse benefits to economically inactive Union citizens.

A comparable idea, also encompassing workers, has been voiced in the political sphere. David Cameron (at that time the UK Prime Minister) was its main proponent, for example with his article in the *Financial Times* of 26 November 2013, significantly entitled 'Free movement within Europe needs to be less free'.[77] For Cameron, 'the concept of free movement [had to return] to a more sensible basis' without Treaty change—hence through changes in case law and/or legislation. Similar worries were expressed in a joint letter sent to the Commission by the interior ministers of the United Kingdom, Germany, Austria, and the Netherlands in April 2013.[78] Insofar as economically inactive citizens are concerned, and regardless of the applicable legal materials, the economic preferences of those Member States were fully reflected in the *Dano* judgment.

From a purely utilitarian perspective, this position makes sense. It is obviously simpler and cheaper for the more prosperous states to refuse social assistance outright, on the basis of an

[77] See www.ft.com/content/add36222-56be-11e3-ab12-00144feabdc0.
[78] See http://docs.dpaq.de/3604-130415_letter_to_presidency_final_1_2.pdf.

automatic and absolute presumption. What they save with *Dano* is the economic burden of the *Grzelczyk* approach as codified in the Citizens' Rights Directive. That burden corresponds to the sum total of the cost of granting social assistance to Union citizens while the burden remains reasonable, of deporting them once the burden becomes unreasonable and they lose their right of residence, and of ensuring that they do not come back without having sufficient resources, plus the administrative cost of the individual assessments required by Union law.

While that overall cost might not be insignificant, in macro-economic terms it is likely to be negligible. Besides, it is not a net cost, as it is clearly set off by the much larger benefits that free movement brings, in general and for social security systems. According to a report requested by the Commission in the wake of the letter from the four interior ministers and issued on 14 October 2013, in most countries Union migrants represent less than 5 per cent of welfare beneficiaries. Moreover, through taxes and other contributions they give much more than they receive in benefits. The study found no evidence that the 'main motivation of [Union] citizens to migrate and reside in a different Member State is benefit-related as opposed to work or family-related'. Contrary to the claims of the four ministers, the report shows that the social security systems of those states benefit considerably from migration.[79]

Economic concerns alone cannot explain *Dano*, which is about symbolic politics through and through. Its driving force is the reassertion of the nation state as the main form of political organization in contemporary Europe and, in consequence, the parallel vindication of national citizenship as the predominant legal status, over and above a crumpled Union citizenship. For the Court, the pressure of this reassertion is coupled with a number of fears: a fear of populism, disaffection and hatred for the Union; a fear of a nationalist retreat in the middle of the

[79] 'A fact finding analysis on the impact on the Member States' social security systems of the entitlements of non-active intra-EU migrants to special non-contributory cash benefits and healthcare granted on the basis of residence' (available at ec.europa.eu/employment_social/empl_portal/facebook/20131014%20GHK%20study%20web_EU%20migration.pdf).

crisis; a fear of the possible breakup and gradual disintegration of the Union; and a fear, even, of an abrupt end to integration and its law.

The overreaction of the Court adjudicating under so much pressure led to a result that seems historically myopic and morally worrying. If the treatment of the other—in particular the most significant other for the original aim of integration, i.e. nationals from other Member States—with regard to assistance aimed at ensuring basic human dignity, is an indicator of the moral shape of integration, with *Dano* we may have reached the lowest watermark since the beginning.

The idea running through the judgment is that the Union legal order will mainly grant protection to those who work—i.e. those who contribute to the economy of the host state. There is a remarkable insistence on this point. We learn that Ms Dano 'has not been trained in a profession', that, 'to date, she has not worked in Germany or Romania', that 'she is not seeking employment and . . . did not enter Germany in order to work'. The Court states, in a rather peculiar fashion, that Union law 'distinguishes between (i) persons who are working and (ii) those who are not'. Besides the moralistic undertones of these passages, we seem to go back to a period in which the Treaty of Maastricht had not been adopted and the free movement rules had not yet been complemented with the non-economic provisions on Union citizenship.

What is more worrying from the perspective of the historical experience that led to integration and of the values underlying it, the judgment considers it a matter of total indifference for Union law that a Member State allows certain nationals of other Member States to remain in its territory as lawful residents while refusing to grant them assistance aimed at allowing them to 'lead a life in keeping with human dignity'. In other words, the Court does not object—indeed, it implies that it has nothing to say about it—to a system of social assistance that secures human dignity for some while treating other lawful residents according to a standard that the state legislature deems to be incompatible with human dignity. The judgment seems to accept that the requirement of human dignity, enshrined as 'inviolable' in Article 1 of the Charter of Fundamental Rights, could vary depending on one's nationality and indeed become irrelevant for the 'losers' of integration, whose presence the more prosperous states could tolerate, considering that those persons may not be totally useless as marginal consumers or as bearers of the future, possibly cheaper, labour force of countries with a problematic demographic curve.

Dano is not only questionable in legal and moral terms. In strategic terms it was a pointless concession. If the Court ever thought that sacrificing Ms Dano and other 'economically inactive' citizens in need could put an end to the strenuous strife of some to reduce the costs of integration, protecting Union workers, this was an elementary mistake in the ongoing 'negotiation'. As regards 'Brexit', we know that the British people voted to leave the Union anyway, in spite of this and other concessions.[80] As regards the Court's authority, this retreat has not prevented further attempts at eroding that authority and the integrity of Union law.

Rather than protecting Union workers, the Court's reversal in *Dano* was immediately followed by an attempt to curb their social rights. That was the main substantive part of the so-called 'new settlement for the United Kingdom within the European Union', now defunct. Some of the demands of the United Kingdom were accepted in part by the remainder Member States, and shared by some of them, and there was a commitment to change existing secondary law to allow the Member States to discriminate against *workers* from other Member States, under certain conditions and for a number of years, with regard to vaguely defined welfare subsidies. The proposed measure was unorthodox from the perspective of primary law, as its justification was weak, to say the least, and its proportionality more than dubious. Some thought that one day in the distant future the Court might object to those changes, but it may be wondered whether the Court would have put at risk the membership of Britain in order to protect the few workers concerned by that measure.

[80] The holdings of *Dano* were reflected in 'A New Settlement for the United Kingdom within the European Union', OJ 2016 CI 69/1, at 8.

With the demise of the 'new settlement for the United Kingdom within the European Union', some may think that the temptation of eroding further the elements of solidarity in the Union system has been averted, but that temptation will be there as long as the economic crisis and the institutional crisis remain the permanent horizon of integration.

The temptation is that of conceiving the Union as a game in which all the states should win all the time and in all sub-games, never losing or conceding anything, engaging in cooperation only when there is something to win, and trying to reduce costs and maintain or recover as much autonomy as possible for the rest, rolling back the policies which entail any sort of solidarity. This conception would deeply transform and undermine the Union. As Erik Eriksen has put it, 'European integration is not only a win-win arrangement; it is not merely a matter of joint convenience and choice, but a matter of justice and solidarity'.[81]

Over the second half of the twentieth century, integration has developed as a system in which all the states are better off in the long run, not only in economic terms but also in social, political, and legal terms, even though they may lose something, sometimes, for the benefit of all. In the utilitarian view of integration, this sense of common responsibility and solidarity disappears. The costs of integration are decoupled from its benefits and are no longer seen as their necessary counterpart. Only direct benefits, such as those received through structural funds, are acknowledged, while the wider benefits due to the internal market and to membership of a peaceful and advanced polity are not taken into account. This is accompanied by a strenuous effort at maximizing benefits while minimizing all costs, an effort that may actually harm the overall economic performance of the Union—and also its recovery from the crisis, hampered by a short-sighted and suboptimal response. This utilitarian approach is one of the symptoms of the current pull towards disintegration, visible in various areas and institutional settings. Its dangers for integration can hardly be overstated, as it negates supranational solidarity, a basic principle of the European project.

[81] Eriksen, *supra* note 2, at 117.

6

FUNDAMENTAL RIGHTS AND THE INTEGRITY OF UNION LAW

1

Another area of the law of integration that is highly controversial and relevant in structural terms is the protection of fundamental rights, in particular regarding the scope and standard of the protection offered at Union level, the consequences for national law, and the implications of the future accession of the Union to the European Convention on Human Rights. These issues may be somewhat less salient in political terms than those connected to citizenship and equality, but they are of fundamental importance for the integrity of Union law and of wider significance for the political understanding of the Union.

This chapter tries to explore these questions in the light of two recent leading decisions: the judgment in *Fransson* and Opinion 2/13.[1] Before analysing the decisions I would like to put them in a broader perspective, outlining the multiple functions of fundamental rights and recalling the genealogy of their protection in the Union.

Like citizenship, fundamental rights are not just a legal matter and a purely legal analysis would be insufficient. It is not possible to grasp the role of fundamental rights in the Union without having first understood the various functions they have in contemporary legal and political systems, and in the international sphere.

The first function, the most obvious one for the jurist, is that of defining in a higher legal plane, shielded from interference by the legislature and by the other constituted powers of a given polity, a protected sphere for the benefit of all those who fall under the law of that polity. The protection of fundamental

[1] *Fransson*, see chapter 5, note 75; Opinion 2/13 of the Court, of 18 December 2014 (EU:C:2014:2454).

What's Left of the Law of Integration? Decay and Resistance in European Union Law. First Edition. Julio Baquero Cruz. © Julio Baquero Cruz 2018. Published 2018 by Oxford University Press.

rights is generally entrusted to the judicial process, as a matter of law. Their effectiveness will thus depend on the existence of a solid rule of law and a strong judiciary. Fundamental rights, enshrined as constitutional rights, are the basic legal mechanism limiting power and preserving the overall fairness of a political system. They are a key element among the various checks and balances shaping contemporary constitutional orders.

Due to their function as a limit to power, fundamental rights are also an important tool of legitimation, which works alongside other elements of the political system, such as elections and democratic representation (input legitimacy) or policies aimed at improving the welfare of the population (output legitimacy).[2] From this perspective, fundamental rights should not be seen as just another instrument used to obtain output legitimacy, since they frame and guide the choices made in all policy sectors. And many fundamental rights, such as freedom of speech, the right to vote in free elections, the right of association, the right to information, or the right to judicial protection, are an indispensable part of the infrastructure of a democracy based on the rule of law, which is only sustainable if they are entrenched and shielded effectively from majoritarian decision-making.

A third important function of fundamental rights relates to the identity of a political community. The rights which are qualified as 'fundamental' provide an ideal representation of that community. They are part of the constitutional culture, real or imagined, of a polity, embodying a reflection of collective values and of the relative weight given to each of them. Compared to other vectors of political identity, such as language, religion, or tradition, fundamental rights have the potential to be more inclusive, promoting a tolerant and open political identity.

In the international sphere, fundamental rights have two additional functions as regards relations between different polities. The first is that of adding another layer of protection to reinforce, with an international normative framework and sometimes also with an external institutional review, the basic content of those rights. The second function is to guarantee the

[2] For this distinction, see F. Scharpf, *Governing in Europe: Effective and Democratic?* (1999).

minimum legitimacy required of a political community if it is to be recognized among its peers as reasonably fair in view of the degree of protection it offers to individuals.[3] These functions are reflected in the idea of *universal human rights* as a minimum threshold of human decency, which is to be distinguished from the more stringent notion of *fundamental rights* as the constitutional basis of a polity.

Finally, in federal, divided-power, or multi-level systems, fundamental rights are often a sensitive field with regard to the tensions between the federation and the federated entities. This is not a function of fundamental rights but a special trait of their protection in those systems. In such a context, all the dimensions of fundamental rights are affected by federal frictions, in particular as regards the respective scopes and levels of protection.

The various functions of fundamental rights are complementary and cannot be neatly divided. They influence each other. The legal dimension frames the political functions, and vice-versa. There is no political and legal system in which only one of the functions is present and not the others.

All these functions are at work in the European Union at present. Although the beginnings of the discourse about fundamental rights in integration were mainly linked to the Communities' assertion of legal autonomy, that discourse was never detached from the themes of limiting power and reinforcing legitimacy, which gained more prominence as integration unfolded. The 'federal question' was always at the heart of the practice of fundamental rights in the Union.[4] As we will see, the tension between the scopes and standards of protection of Union law and national constitutional law was visible in the very first cases decided by the Court on these matters. And the external international function of minimum protection is also relevant for the Union, with its envisaged accession to the European Convention on Human Rights.

[3] For this conception, see J. Rawls, *The Law of Peoples* (2001).

[4] See P. Eeckhout, 'The EU Charter of Fundamental Rights and the Federal Question', *Common Market Law Review* (2002) 945.

2

A brief overview of the process through which fundamental rights became part of the law of integration may help us understand the current situation and the full significance of the Court's recent decisions in this field.

One should nuance, first of all, the conventional view, according to which fundamental rights were totally absent from the founding Treaties. While they contained no comprehensive catalogue of fundamental rights, it is inaccurate to say they were wholly silent in that regard. To begin with, they included the free movement rules, which are the building blocks of a fundamental right to pursue economic activities in cross-border situations. Secondly, they contained the provisions concerning the procedures before the European Court of Justice, which flesh out the fundamental right to judicial protection. Thirdly, there was a general provision on non-discrimination on grounds of nationality, specified in the various economic and social free movement rules, which is comparable to a fundamental right to equality on those grounds. And, finally, there was the provision on gender equality with regard to pay and other working conditions, whose fundamental character is equally hard to deny.[5]

On the other hand, the absence of a comprehensive catalogue of fundamental rights seems understandable in the historical context of the 1950s, in view of the limited scope of the Communities and of the division of work in the post-war effort to reconstruct the legal and political structures of Western Europe. The issue of fundamental rights had been dealt with in national constitutions and, at a supranational level, in the framework of the Council of Europe, with the European Convention on Human Rights of 1950 and the European Court of Human Rights established in 1959. It would have been odd for the drafters to repeat the same exercise in the framework of the European Coal and Steel Community and of the European Economic Community and Euratom, with their predominantly economic objectives. The drafters might have thought that the

[5] This argument had previously been made by P. Pescatore in 'Les droits de l'homme et l'intégration européenne', *Cahiers de droit européen* (1968) 627, at 645–8.

few provisions mentioned earlier were sufficient. In contrast, Article 3 of the statute of the unborn European Political Community provided that the provisions of the European Convention on Human Rights would have become an integral part of that organization, and Article 43 thereof granted the Court of Justice the competence to apply them.[6]

Time proved that the drafters were a bit short-sighted in this area. In spite of the few fundamental provisions already mentioned, in the 1960s and 1970s the absence of a catalogue of fundamental rights in the founding Treaties became problematic for the basic features of the law of integration. In Germany and Italy, the defeated countries in which strong constitutional courts had been created and entrusted with the protection of fundamental rights, this gap prompted a lively judicial and academic debate about whether it was legitimate to transfer powers to the Communities without ensuring the protection of fundamental rights, and about whether national constitutions were bound to fill in that gap in the shared system of law.

In Germany, the main laboratory for this line of case law, the positions were far from unanimous. While the national court referring the preliminary question in *Internationale Handelsgesellschaft* claimed that the German Basic Law applied and that some provisions of secondary Community law were incompatible with it,[7] the referring court in *Stauder* simply asked whether the relevant Community provision complied with the general principles of Community law.[8] Similarly, the referring court in *Köster* considered that the principles of economic freedom and proportionality 'which are intended to guarantee protection of fundamental rights form an integral part of both international law and the supranational legal order, such that a Community measure contrary to these concepts must be considered null

[6] *Ibid.*, at 630.

[7] *Internationale Handelsgesellschaft*, see chapter 2, note 9, at para. 2: 'the Verwaltungsgericht has until now refused to accept the validity of the provisions in question', considering that 'the primacy of supranational law must yield before the principles of the German Basic Law'.

[8] Case 29/69, *Stauder*, EU:C:1969:57, at 420 and 412.

and void'.[9] In a similar vein, in the latter case the European Commission proposed an approach that would allow protection of fundamental rights while preserving the autonomy of the law of integration: 'the Community institutions are bound by Community law alone and in their regard the protection conferred by the fundamental rights of national constitutions flows only from Community law, written or unwritten'.[10]

There were two possible avenues for tackling the structural issue: to fill in the gap with national constitutional law, a solution that could undermine the law of integration, or to fill it within the Community system, respecting its autonomy but running the parallel risk of compromising the national systems of fundamental rights protection.

As though to remind us of the roots of integration, the first significant case in which the Court addressed this matter, *Stauder*, of 1969, concerned a beneficiary of a welfare scheme for those disabled in the war.[11] The scheme, established by the European Economic Community, gave access to cheaper butter to those persons, but it seemed to require a voucher with the name of the beneficiary. As stated above, the referring German court had doubts about whether the scheme respected fundamental rights, which it suggested should be protected as general principles of Community law.

In its judgment, the Court interpreted the applicable rule in such a way that the fundamental rights problem vanished as a matter of Community law, while avoiding any potential conflict with national constitutional law. For the Court, the relevant provision of secondary law did not require or prohibit 'the identification of beneficiaries by name'. Each Member State was 'able to choose from a number of methods by which the coupons may refer to the person concerned'.[12] In other words, if there was any interference with fundamental rights, it was not due to the provision of Community law but to its implementation in Germany. The problem could thus be left to German law. Hence the conclusion: 'the provision at issue contain[ed]

[9] Case 25/70, *Köster*, EU:C:1970:115, at para. 21.
[10] *Ibid.*, at 1167. [11] *Stauder*, *supra* note 8, at 421.
[12] *Ibid.*, at para. 6.

nothing capable of prejudicing the fundamental human rights enshrined in the general principles of Community law and protected by the Court'.[13]

This timid conclusion contains part of the answer to the structural issue mentioned earlier. Following the position of the referring court, the Court states that fundamental rights can be protected as general principles of Community law, using its own institutions and procedures. Note, however, that no reason is given to justify this position and that the judgment is silent about whether national constitutional systems or the European Convention on Human Rights could have a parallel role in granting such protection.

In a rudimentary fashion, *Stauder* also touches upon the thorny issue of the scope of application of Community fundamental rights when a state acts within the scope of Community law. The position of the judgment seems to be that those fundamental rights would only be relevant if the validity of Community law is at stake—be it directly or through an action against the national act implementing it. When the interference with a fundamental right is due to a free choice made by a Member State in the framework of its implementation of Community law, and the validity of the latter is not at stake, there would be no reason for Community law to apply and the issue could be left to state law.

This approach to the scope of Union fundamental rights could seem reasonable at first sight. From a wider perspective, however, it could be considered that the national implementing provisions only existed to give effect to the obligation established by the Commission Decision, and that if they were to be reviewed pursuant to national fundamental rights, although that review could not directly affect the validity of secondary Community law, it could hamper, at least temporarily, its uniform and effective implementation. From this perspective, the Court could have claimed a role to review, vis-à-vis Community fundamental rights, the measures adopted by a Member State in the framework of the implementation of Community

[13] *Ibid.*, at para. 7.

law, even in situations in which the problematic aspect of the national measure was not fully determined by that law.

The Court gave a more complete expression of its position about a year later, in *Internationale Handelsgesellschaft*. In that case, the referring court questioned the validity of two provisions of secondary Community law regarding the common organization of the market in cereals. According to those provisions, the award of export licences was conditional on the lodging of a deposit guaranteeing that the exportation would take place during the relevant period. If the cereals were not exported at all or only partially, all or part of the deposit would be lost. The referring court considered that those rules constituted an excessive interference with 'certain structural principles of national constitutional law [freedom of action and of disposition, economic liberty and proportionality] which must be protected within the framework of Community law, with the result that the primacy of supranational law must yield before the principles of the German Basic Law'.[14]

As in *Stauder*, the preliminary questions were about the validity of secondary Community law in the light of fundamental rights. By contrast, in *Internationale Handelsgesellschaft* the interference was the direct consequence of Community law and not of a discretionary decision taken by a Member State in the framework of its implementation. In addition, the referring court did not propose protecting fundamental rights as a matter of Community law, but suggested using national constitutional law to override the primacy of Community law.

The Court of Justice stated its position in two very clear paragraphs. The first one excludes the possibility of using national fundamental rights to review Community law:

> Recourse to the legal rules or concepts of national law in order to judge the validity of measures adopted by the institutions of the Community would have an adverse effect on the uniformity and efficacy of Community law. The validity of such measures can only be judged in the light of Community law. In fact, the law stemming from the Treaty, an independent source of law, cannot because of its very nature be overridden by rules of national law, however framed,

[14] *Internationale Handelsgesellschaft*, see chapter 2, note 9, at para. 2.

without being deprived of its character as Community law and without the legal basis of the Community itself being called in question. Therefore the validity of a Community measure or its effect within a Member State cannot be affected by allegations that it runs counter to either fundamental rights as formulated by the constitution of that State or the principles of a national constitutional structure.[15]

Building on *Stauder*, this negative step is followed by a positive statement announcing comparable safeguards within the Community system:

However, an examination should be made as to whether or not any analogous guarantee inherent in Community law has been disregarded. In fact, respect for fundamental rights forms an integral part of the general principles of law protected by the Court of Justice. The protection of such rights, whilst inspired by the constitutional traditions common to the Member States, must be ensured within the framework of the structure and objectives of the Community. . . .[16]

The Court did not develop this line of case law because it considered that there were shortcomings in the protection of fundamental rights at national level. Indeed, it stated that the protection of fundamental rights as general principles of Community law would find inspiration in the common constitutional traditions of the states. Its main objective was to preserve the autonomy, primacy, uniformity, and effectiveness of the law of integration. Its direct source is *Costa v. ENEL*, which had already made clear that the legality of Community law could not be reviewed vis-à-vis national law.[17] This explains the Court's decision to draw a neat line between situations falling within the scope of Community law, which would be subject to review in respect of Community fundamental rights, excluding any parallel review pursuant to national fundamental rights, and other situations, which would remain subject to national law.

That line is not drawn in the place suggested by *Stauder*. From that judgment one could have deduced that Community fundamental rights were only relevant when the validity of a Community act was contested directly or indirectly, leaving the remainder

[15] *Ibid.*, at para. 3. [16] *Ibid.*, at para. 4.
[17] *Costa v. ENEL*, see chapter 2, note 7.

for national constitutional law. In *Internationale Handelsgesellschaft* the Court cast a wider net for the law of integration, as it asserted a Community review, excluding national review, not only in situations in which the validity of a Community measure is at stake but also in cases in which *its effect within a Member State* could be affected by the application of fundamental rights. This broader formulation renders Community fundamental rights applicable to all situations falling within the scope of the law of integration, including those concerning specific national measures taken within that scope, and seemingly regardless of the discretion left to the Member States.

Beyond these structural aspects, which were the driving force behind the judgment, the approach of *Internationale Handelsgesellschaft* may be seen as a positive asset for the legitimacy of the Community. Complementing direct effect and primacy, the Court of Justice asserted its role in protecting not only the individual rights expressly granted by the Treaty and by Community legislation, but also the fundamental rights that may be breached by Community secondary law. This reduces the possibility of using Community law in unacceptable ways and tends to reinforce its legitimacy, constraining the powers of the institutions. Finally, with its reference to '*common* constitutional traditions', this case law is an initial step towards an overarching European identity. As suggested, fundamental rights are sustained by common values and project an ideal representation of a political community. Excluding review under national constitutional law and asserting its own review 'within the framework of the structure and objectives of the Community', the Court of Justice implied that it is possible and desirable to define, within the area of integration, a common European approach to the complex and far-reaching issues raised by fundamental rights.

The legal reasons behind this case law and its wider implications should lead us to reconsider the conventional view, according to which it would have been the German Constitutional Court which gently pushed the European Court of Justice to develop its fundamental rights jurisprudence, in a virtuous episode of 'constitutional pluralism' and of informal dialogue between courts. Ulrich Everling recalls that the relevant line of case law of the Court of Justice predated *Solange I*. He also argues that it was 'an odd supposition that the personalities who were or are judges of the Court of Justice are squinting timidly at the judgment of a German or other national court and that they can be influenced by pressures of national institutions. According to my experience, the judges are never impressed if national courts even of the highest level threaten to ignore their obligations under the Treaty'.[18] As we have seen, the idea of protecting fundamental rights as general principles of Community law was voiced by some German courts, in a period in which the German Constitutional Court was very respectful of integration and rather deferential towards the European Court of Justice.[19]

It seems more accurate to see this development as a natural internal requirement of the law of integration, and as a consequence of the principles of direct effect and primacy. The German debate among lower courts prompted this development at a particular point in time and in particular circumstances, but it is likely that a similar jurisprudence would have developed sooner or later in any event. The idea that Community law constituted a legal order entailed a claim to autonomy and completeness. It meant that its gaps had to be filled in within that order, with its own normative resources. The well-known technique of general principles, deduced from the Treaties and from the common constitutional traditions of the states, was a reasonable choice with which to complete the system while preserving its integrity.

This tends to confirm that there has never been any trade-off between integration and fundamental rights. The solution devised by the Court of Justice achieved both objectives, protecting fundamental rights as part of the supranational rule of law. The frictions leading to this case law were about something else. As with the general resistance to primacy explored in chapter 3, they reflected an institutional struggle for power and

[18] U. Everling, 'The Maastricht Judgment of the German Federal Constitutional Court and its Significance for the Development of the European Union', *Yearbook of European Law* (1994) 1, at 14 and 15.

[19] See chapter 3, section 2, and the order of the German Constitutional Court of 18 October 1967, chapter 3, note 2.

influence, and the underlying tense relationship between the national and supranational elements at work in the legal reconstruction of post-war Europe. Those tensions did not disappear with *Internationale Handelsgesellschaft*, which is more a beginning than an ending in the story of fundamental rights and integration.

3

Indeed, the position of *Internationale Handelsgesellschaft* on the basic architecture of fundamental rights protection in the Community was not accepted by the referring court. Defying the authority of the European Court of Justice, on 24 November 1971 that national court referred similar questions on the same case to the German Constitutional Court. This led to the *Solange I* judgment of 29 May 1974.[20]

For the referring court, European Community law was 'not entitled to take precedence over all national law' and could be reviewed against the Basic Law.[21] By contrast, in its submission to the German Constitutional Court, the German ministry of justice held that the reference was inadmissible, in view of previous case law according to which no direct review of Community acts was possible in constitutional complaints.[22]

Before addressing the main legal issue, the German Constitutional Court made two preliminary points. First, it clarified that the case concerned provisions of secondary Community law whose implementation was 'in the hands of administrative authorities in the Federal Republic of Germany'.[23] It gave no significance to the fact that those authorities did not have any margin of discretion, since they were bound by Community law to forfeit the deposit in proportion to the unused part of the licence. The Constitutional Court seemed to consider that the legality of any act of any German authority should be open to review under the German Basic Law, even when it is fully determined by Community law—which means that its review entails an indirect review of Community law. Secondly, the

[20] BVerfGE, 37, 271; English translation in *The Relationship between European Community Law and National Law*, Volume 1, see chapter 3, note 2, 443.

[21] *Ibid.*, at 443. [22] *Ibid.*, at 444. [23] *Ibid.*, at 445.

German Court expressly left aside two issues: whether the Treaty itself may enter into conflict with provisions of the Basic Law, and whether Community law may clash with other provisions of the Basic Law, beyond fundamental rights.

The case was thus limited to a decision about whether the fundamental rights enshrined in the German Basic Law applied in cases concerning administrative acts of German authorities taken for the implementation of Community secondary law. In that regard, while a minority of three judges of the chamber deciding the case wrote dissenting opinions to defend the integrity of Community law as interpreted by the Court of Justice,[24] a majority of five judges asserted a provisional power of review, to be exercised as long as the Community did not have its own catalogue of fundamental rights, enacted by an elected Parliament, which would be considered adequate when compared with the fundamental rights enshrined in the German Basic Law. In such circumstances, any German court could refer the matter to the Constitutional Court after having obtained a preliminary ruling from the Court of Justice.[25] After this doctrinal elaboration, when it came to the substance of the case the German Court carried out a rather quick review, with a legal assessment that was almost identical to the analysis of the Court of Justice, and concluded that there was no breach of national fundamental rights. A concrete legal clash was thus carefully avoided.

Solange I reads as an ambivalent judicial intervention. From an institutional perspective, the judgment could be seen as the initial episode in a long quest for legal supremacy and institutional pre-eminence in post-war Europe. The statement would be regarded as less about fundamental rights than about the definition of the scope and nature of the respective legal orders and jurisdictions. From that point of view, while a role was preserved for the European Court of Justice, the German Court wanted to keep the last word for itself. *Solange I* would thus prefigure the future position of the German Court as the guardian of the legitimacy of the nation state and of its supposedly stronger political identity.

[24] *Ibid.*, at 452–60. [25] *Ibid.*, at 447–52.

From a legal point of view, it could however be argued that, in spite of the lack of disagreement about the case in hand, the German Court could have legitimate concerns about the ability of the Court of Justice to properly protect fundamental rights in the absence of a clear source in Community law and in view of its limited experience in that field. These shortcomings could justify its decision to preserve the competence granted to it by the German Basic Law.

One perspective does not necessarily exclude the other, but it is worth recalling that *Solange I* presents a provisional and flexible position. The main driving force behind the judgment is legal certainty. The Constitutional Court considered that a jurisprudence based on general principles, without a clear textual basis, could not ensure the required legal certainty. Until that certainty is achieved, the German Court would offer its protection to those falling within the scope of the Basic Law. One could therefore deduce from *Solange I* that once the Community had its own catalogue of fundamental rights the Constitutional Court would conclude that Community law, as interpreted by the Court of Justice, would no longer be subject to constitutional limits in Germany. Even though a degree of anxiety about legal influence and boundaries transpires from *Solange I*, we are very far away from the positions that the German Court would take after the 1990s to defend the supposedly more legitimate national democracy, the essence of state powers, or the immutable national 'constitutional identity'.

After 1974 the European Court of Justice continued to develop its fundamental rights jurisprudence without actually being subject to the strict oversight announced in *Solange I*. The Court made clear that its case law on fundamental rights as general principles of Community law would not only draw inspiration from the constitutional traditions common to the Member States but also from international treaties signed by those states, among which the European Convention on Human Rights, and the attendant jurisprudence of the Strasbourg Court, would have a special significance.[26] The Court also confirmed that Community

[26] Case 4/73, *Nold v. Commission*, EU:C:1974:51, at para. 13; and Case 44/79, *Hauer*, EU:C:1979:290, at para. 15.

fundamental rights are not only binding on the European institutions but also on the Member States when they adopt measures falling within the scope of Community law, whether this be for the implementation of that law, even if state authorities are granted a margin of discretion, or by derogating from it, as with the exceptions to the free movement rules.[27] And it reassured Member States that it would always provide a high standard of protection, being 'bound to draw inspiration from constitutional traditions common to the Member States', and unable to 'uphold measures which are incompatible with fundamental rights recognised and guaranteed by the Constitutions of those States'.[28]

Throughout these judgments, the baseline remained the need to ensure the autonomy, primacy, uniformity, and effectiveness of the law of integration. And yet one wonders how effective the case law ever was in doing so. As in other fields of Community law and perhaps even more, it is likely that judicial practice in the Member States was not strictly compliant with the preliminary rulings procedure, and that the Court only dealt with a small part of the fundamental rights claims falling within the scope of Community law that should have reached it.

On 22 October 1986, the German Constitutional Court returned to a more deferential position in the so-called *Solange II* judgment,[29] prompted by a constitutional complaint about a case that had been referred to and decided by the European Court of Justice (the *Wünsche* case).[30] After a long and complex reasoning, the German Court held as follows:

[S]o long as the European Communities, and in particular the case law of the European Court, generally ensure an effective protection of fundamental rights as against the sovereign powers of the Communities

[27] Joined Cases 60/84 and 61/84, *Cinéthèque*, EU:C:1985:329, at para. 26; Case 222/84, *Johnston*, EU:C:1986:206, at para. 18; Case 12/86, *Demirel*, EU: C:1987:400, at para. 28; Case 5/88, *Wachauf*, EU:C:1989:321, at paras. 19 and 22; and Case 260/89, *ERT*, EU:C:1991:254, at paras. 41–5.

[28] *Nold*, *supra* note 26, at para. 13.

[29] BVerfGE 73, 339; English translation in *The Relationship between European Community Law and National Law*, Volume 1, see chapter 3, note 2.

[30] Case 145/81, *Wünsche*, EU:C:1982:254.

> which is to be regarded as substantially similar to the protection of fundamental rights required unconditionally by the [Basic Law], and in so far as they generally safeguard the essential content of fundamental rights, the Federal Constitutional Court will no longer exercise its jurisdiction to decide on the applicability of secondary Community legislation cited as the legal basis for any acts of German courts or authorities within the sovereign jurisdiction of the Federal Republic of Germany, and it will no longer review such legislation by the standard of the fundamental rights contained in the Basic Law.[31]

The main reasons given for this change were: the gradual consolidation of the fundamental rights case law of the Court of Justice; the statement in *Nold*, which for the German Court meant that national fundamental rights were 'obligatory standards for reviewing measures of Community organs taken within their spheres of jurisdiction';[32] the statement that the Court would always try 'to ensure the best possible development of any particular principle of fundamental rights in Community law'; the fundamental rights declarations adopted by the Community institutions in 1977 and 1978; and the central role that the European Convention on Human Rights had started to play in the jurisprudence of the Court of Justice.[33]

This was a remarkable reversal. At least one of the strict conditions laid down in *Solange I*, the requirement of a catalogue adopted 'by a parliament and of settled validity', was not satisfied. The change seems to concede that the jurisprudence of the Court of Justice was sufficient to provide adequate protection, even though it was based on unwritten general principles. The decision not to insist on the adoption of an unambiguous textual basis seems correct, as fundamental rights provisions are very open-textured and it is only through case law that they may become more precise. Besides the grounds given by the German Constitutional Court, *Solange II* has an obvious political context.

[31] BVerfGE 73, 339; English translation in *The Relationship between European Community Law and National Law*, Volume 1, see chapter 3, note 2, at 494.

[32] *Ibid.*, at 489.

[33] *Ibid.*, at 489–94. The judgment refers to the Joint Declaration by the European Parliament, the Council and the Commission, of 5 April 1977, on fundamental rights (OJ 1977 C 103/1); and to the European Council statement on democracy of 7 and 8 April 1978 (*Bulletin EC* 3-1978, at 5 and 6).

It was in 1986—the year of the entry into force of the Single European Act, opening a very dynamic period for the Community after a long period of stagnation—that the German Court concluded that there was no trade-off between integration and fundamental rights, and that the latter could be sufficiently guaranteed within the European system.

The reversal, however, was not complete. First of all, the German Court did not totally renounce its power of review. It simply stated that it would not exercise it 'as long as' Community law and the case law of the Court of Justice ensured a protection of fundamental rights that was generally comparable to the one it itself granted pursuant to the German Basic Law. Secondly, the judgment followed the perspective of German constitutional law, and its reasoning did not coincide with that of the Court of Justice. Finally, the conditional eclipse of the jurisdiction of the German Court was limited to the review of 'secondary Community legislation', i.e. to acts adopted by the Union institutions. The language of *Solange II* suggests that the German Court would continue exercising its jurisdiction as regards acts of the German courts or authorities falling within the scope of Community law, at least as long as reviewing them would not amount to an indirect review of the legality of Community legislation, i.e. as long as the acts under review were a discretionary decision of national authorities, not fully determined by Community law.

That deferential but vigilant position has been maintained by the German Constitutional Court to the present day.[34] Accordingly, that Court declares inadmissible any constitutional complaint brought against Union acts for breaches of fundamental rights enshrined in the German Basic Law, as it considers that the protection granted by Union law through the Court of Justice is roughly equivalent. The only exception is Article 38 of the German Basic Law, on the fundamental right to vote in democratic

[34] See, for example, the 'Maastricht decision' of 12 October 1993, see chapter 3, note 7; the order of 7 June 2000, BVerfGE 102, 147; English translation in *The Relationship between European Community Law and National Law*, Volume 2, see chapter 3, note 2, at 270–85; and the 'Lisbon decision' of 30 June 2009 (2 BvE 2/08, DE:BVerfG:2009: es20090630.2bve000208), at para. 191.

elections, which constitutes the wide basis for the current case law of the German Court, focused on the review of manifest and structurally significant breaches of the limits of Union powers, and more generally on the protection of essential state powers and 'constitutional identity'.[35]

The most significant subsequent developments did not occur in the judicial arena but in the Treaties. Article F(2) of the Treaty of Maastricht codified the fundamental rights case law of the Court of Justice as follows: 'The Union shall respect fundamental rights, as guaranteed by the European Convention for the Protection of Human Rights and Fundamental Freedoms signed in Rome on 4 November 1950 and as they result from the constitutional traditions common to the Member States, as general principles of Community law.' Other fundamental right provisions, such as those on Union citizenship, the right of access to documents or the right to good administration, were gradually inserted into the Treaties. Then came the Charter of Fundamental Rights of the European Union, granted legal effect as primary law by the Treaty of Lisbon, and binding on the institutions, bodies, offices, and agencies of the Union, and also on the Member States when they implement Union law. The Treaty of Lisbon also instructed the Union to accede to the European Convention on Human Rights.

The circle seemed to be closed and many might have thought that the tensions around fundamental rights and integration were about to end. Paradoxically, rather than solving them the prominence of the Charter has revived these tensions, adding an additional layer of complexity.

As a matter of practice, one has the impression that the Charter is not always applied as it should be when it comes to state action taken within the scope of Union law. Most Union law is implemented by state authorities, and their acts, even if they are partly or fully determined by Union law, will usually be

[35] For a summary, see the order of the German Constitutional Court of 14 January 2014 in the *Gauweiler* case (2 BvR 2728/13, DE:BVerfG:2014:rs20140114.2bvr272813), at paras. 17–32. On the limits of *ultra vires* review, see the order of 6 July 2010 in the *Honeywell* case (2 BvR 2661/06, DE:BVerfG:2010:rs20100706.2br266106).

reviewed by national judges vis-à-vis national fundamental rights. Disregarding the principle of equivalence, the national procedures for the enforcement of fundamental rights are rarely applied to enforce Charter rights when a situation falls within the scope of Union law. Besides, if the preliminary rulings procedure is not rigorously respected by national courts of last resort, the situation could lead to a lack of uniformity in the actual interpretation and application of Union law.

As a matter of theory, the relevant legal issues are no longer the same, since the exclusive power of the Court of Justice to review the legality of Union acts with regard to fundamental rights is no longer under discussion. The remaining tensions concern other themes: the extent of the applicability of the Charter to state action falling within the scope of Union law; the possible parallel application of state fundamental rights to such action, and its limits; and the legal questions surrounding the process of accession of the Union to the European Convention on Human Rights. The first two issues are at the heart of the judgment in *Fransson*, to which we now turn.

4

Mr Åkerberg Fransson was charged with serious offences regarding income tax and value added tax before a Swedish court. The tax authorities had already imposed upon him an administrative sanction, which he did not challenge. The national criminal court sent a preliminary reference to the Court of Justice asking whether the charges brought against him should be dismissed in view of the prohibition on being punished twice for the same facts laid down in Article 50 of the Charter, since he had already been punished with the administrative sanction.

As a preliminary matter, the Swedish, Czech, Danish, Irish, and Dutch governments and the Commission questioned the admissibility of the reference. They all argued that the penalties and charges concerning Mr Åkerberg Fransson were outside the scope of the Charter, claiming that they did not constitute an implementation of Union law. Their argument was based on the wording of Article 51(1) of the Charter, which, in their view, had narrowed down the scope of application of Union fundamental rights. As general principles of Union law, those rights applied whenever the states acted 'within the scope of Union law', while Article 51(1) of the Charter provides that its provisions are addressed to those states 'only when they are implementing Union law'.

The judgment curtly rejected this argument. For the Court, Article 51(1) of the Charter simply 'confirms the Court's case law relating to the extent to which actions of the Member States must comply with the requirements flowing from the fundamental rights guaranteed in the legal order of the European Union'. According to that case law, Union fundamental rights apply 'in all situations governed by European Union law, but not outside such situations'. This interpretation is in line with the explanations relating to the Charter, which clarified that that provision was meant to reflect the case law of the Court. As a result, '[t]he applicability of European Union law entails the applicability of the fundamental rights guaranteed by the Court'. The Court only lacks jurisdiction regarding situations which do not come within the scope of Union law.[36]

The Court then moved on to assess whether, on the facts, the situation was within the scope of Union law. The judgment recalled that the penalties and charges regarding Mr Åkerberg Fransson concerned in part value added tax, which is subject to Union legislation which binds the Member States to ensure collection and prevent evasion with appropriate measures. In addition, part of that tax constitutes a resource of the Union's budget and Article 325 TFEU binds those states 'to counter illegal activities affecting the financial interests of the European Union through effective deterrent measures and, in particular, . . . to take the same measures to counter fraud affecting the financial interests of the European Union as they take to counter fraud affecting their own interests'. Even though those penalties and charges were not a direct implementation of Union legislation, their application aimed to fulfil those obligations.[37] As a

[36] *Fransson*, see chapter 5, note 75, at paras. 18–22 of the judgment.
[37] *Ibid.*, at paras. 24–31.

result, the case concerned an 'implementation' of Union law within the meaning of Article 51(1) of the Charter.

The Court followed with the key paragraph of the judgment, which reflects a new understanding of the architecture of fundamental rights protection in the Union:

> where a court of a Member State is called upon to review whether fundamental rights are complied with by a national provision or measure which, in a situation where action of the Member State is not entirely determined by European Union law, implements the latter for the purpose of Article 51(1) of the Charter, national authorities and courts remain free to apply national standards of protection of fundamental rights, provided that the level of protection provided by the Charter, as interpreted by the Court, and the primacy, unity and effectiveness of European Union law are not thereby compromised.[38]

The remaining part of the judgment which is of interest here is the fundamental rights review. Curiously enough, after asserting the applicability of the Charter and its own jurisdiction the Court seems to have little to say on substance. It first notes that 'Article 50 of the Charter does not preclude a Member State from imposing, for the same acts of non-compliance with declaration obligations in the field of [value added tax], a combination of tax penalties and criminal penalties'. It is 'only if the tax penalty is criminal in nature for the purposes of Article 50 of the Charter and has become final that that provision precludes criminal proceedings in respect of the same acts from being brought against the same person'. For the Court, 'three criteria are relevant for the purpose of assessing whether tax penalties are criminal in nature': 'the legal classification of the offence under national law, . . . the very nature of the offence, and . . . the nature and degree of severity of the penalty that the person concerned is liable to incur'. Depending on the circumstances of each case, an administrative sanction may be considered criminal for the purposes of Article 50 of the Charter, precluding criminal proceedings for the same facts. With this rather general guidance, the Court leaves it to the referring court to determine whether

[38] *Ibid.*, at para. 29, referring to Case C-399/11, *Melloni*, EU:C:2013:107, at para. 60.

that provision has been breached and whether the case 'should be examined in relation to the national standards [of fundamental rights protection], which could lead it, as the case may be, to regard their combination as contrary to those standards, as long as the remaining penalties are effective, proportionate and dissuasive'.[39]

These aspects of the judgment call for a reflection from the perspective of the questions addressed in this chapter.

The first part, on the notion of 'implementation' within the meaning of Article 51(1) of the Charter, reacts to the pressures to which the law of integration is confronted at present. Proposing a restrictive interpretation of the scope of the Charter, the five Member States submitting observations and the Commission were not only advancing a legal argument: they were making a political statement, in tune with the powerful contemporary forces that push for a downsizing of the law of integration and for a corresponding reassertion of the Member States and their legal systems, regardless of the effects on the integrity of Union law.

It is interesting to note that the Court's rejection of those claims was exclusively based on precedent and on the explanations of the Charter, i.e. on historical or original interpretation. The judgment did not pause to mention the problem with the word 'implementation', nor did it use the contextual and teleological arguments that could have strengthened its reasoning. Indeed, in view of Article 6 TEU the binding force of the Charter does not exclude the application of the case law on fundamental rights as general principles of Union law, with their traditional scope—coterminous to that of Union law. It would have been contradictory to draw a narrower scope of application for the Charter, which applies in parallel. Secondly, the Court could have recalled the teleological argument of *Internationale Handelsgesellschaft*: reviewing situations falling within the scope of Union law against national fundamental rights, even when those cases concern state action taken within that scope, could harm the primacy, uniformity, and effectiveness of Union law. With its short and apodictic reasoning, *Fransson* implied, perhaps,

[39] *Fransson*, see chapter 5, note 75, at paras. 34–7.

that the response was so obvious that it did not require a full restatement of the grounds justifying fundamental rights protection in the system of integration.

With its interpretation of the term 'implementation', *Fransson* shows vigorous resistance to decay in Union law, but the issues concerning the scope of the Charter as regards state action are far from settled. That this remains a contentious area may be deduced from a passage in a judgment of the German Constitutional Court rendered while the ink of *Fransson* was still fresh. The German Court held that, to avoid being considered *ultra vires*, *Fransson* 'must not be understood and applied in such a way that absolutely any connection of a provision's subject matter to the merely abstract scope of Union law, or merely incidental effects on Union law, would be sufficient for binding the Member States by the Union's fundamental rights set forth in the [Charter]'.[40]

These reservations lead us to the second aspect of the judgment which requires further reflection. After equating state 'implementation' of Union law with 'State action within the scope of Union law', it is still necessary to determine whether the state is acting within that scope. In some cases this will be a simple matter, but in other cases the elusive character of the boundaries of Union law could render the task very tricky. As already suggested, this assessment can be approached in two different ways. The first would consist in deciding whether the actual interference with the legal position of the fundamental rights holder is due to an act of a Member State adopted within the scope of Union law. The second would only include within the scope of the Charter those cases in which the interference is caused by Union law itself, directly or indirectly, excluding situations in which the Member States had a discretionary choice and could implement Union law without affecting fundamental rights.

According to the first approach, in *Fransson* Union law bound the Member States to provide for effective and deterrent sanctions, with the consequence that those sanctions would also fall

[40] Judgment of 24 April 2013, Case 1 BvR 1215/07, DE:BVerfG:2013: rs20130424. 1vbr12507, at para. 91.

within the scope of Union law—regardless of the wide margin the states have in establishing them.

The second approach would have led to a different result. Union law requires effective and deterrent sanctions, but it does not bind the states to use a combination of administrative and criminal penalties, and even less a combination that could breach the *ne bis in idem* principle. That was the free choice of Sweden, not really resulting from Union law. The situation would have fallen outside the scope of the Charter. Following this approach, fundamental rights review would have to be undertaken pursuant to Swedish law.

This national review would have no direct bearing on the validity of Union law, but in some cases it could compromise its uniformity and effectiveness. If the Swedish court decided that there was a breach of the fundamental right in view of the importance of the administrative penalty, then the criminal sanction would be excluded. If the administrative penalty was not sufficiently effective and dissuasive on its own, that could bring the applicable sanctions below the requirements of Union law. Sweden would then be in breach of Union law and might need to revisit its system of sanctions for value added tax offences for future cases, but this finding would have no consequences for Mr Åkerberg Fransson or other suspects, and so would not ensure immediate effectiveness.

This potential result led the Court to follow the first approach, in line with previous case law.[41] This approach has clear advantages: its application is simpler, it casts a wider net for the Charter, and the risks for the uniformity and effectiveness of Union law are reduced.

At the same time the Court recognizes that the situation in *Fransson* was one 'where action of the Member State *is not entirely determined by European Union law*', i.e. a large measure of discretion was left to the states. For such cases, the Court of Justice nuances its traditional position to allow for the application of higher national standards of review, on condition that

[41] See *Wachauf*, *supra* note 27, Case C-2/92, *Bostock*, EU:C:1994:116, at para. 16, and Joined Cases C-20/00 and C-64/00, *Booker*, EU:C:2003:397, at para. 88.

'the primacy, unity and effectiveness of European Union law are not thereby compromised'. By contrast, where a situation is fully determined by Union law only the Charter applies, leaving no room for the application of national fundamental rights.[42] This distinction is understandable. In cases of full determination, what is actually being reviewed is Union law, not national law—which only reflects the former. In cases of partial determination, national law retains a degree of autonomy and the Charter does not fully displace national fundamental rights, but the Court of Justice frames their application in order to safeguard the integrity of Union law.

The Court is thus introducing a limited exception to one of the central holdings of *Internationaler Handelsgesellschaft*, where a neat line divided the mutually exclusive scopes of application of Community and national fundamental rights—for all cases. The basis for this development is Article 53 of the Charter, construed as a mediating mechanism for situations falling under both Union law and national law. This concurrent application seems better adapted to such hybrid cases, which are very common in contemporary Europe. Indeed, in most fields a complex blend of Union law and national law seems to be the rule rather than the exception, making it very difficult to identify a single source for interferences with fundamental rights.

For all its advantages, this approach is not without problems. In practical terms it is extremely complex. Legal actors need to assess whether the incidence on Union law is sufficient for a case to fall within the scope of that law, and whether the applicable Union rules are so comprehensive as to exclude the parallel application of national fundamental rights. In overlapping areas, those actors should identify the respective levels of protection and, if the national standard turns out to be more protective, determine whether the primacy, unity, and effectiveness of Union law would be harmed by that standard. This series of assessments entails some legal uncertainty, as the rights holders do not know in advance which rules will protect their fundamental rights, and through which procedures.

[42] *Melloni*, *supra* note 38.

Secondly, the acceptance of the concurrent application of national standards in cases of 'partial determination' entails a risk of serious constitutional frictions in the overlapping area. A clear example is the preliminary reference of the Italian Constitutional Court in the *M.A.S. and M.B.* case, following the judgment in *Taricco*.[43] In that reference, the Italian Constitutional Court sought to assert the principle of legality in criminal matters enshrined in the Italian Constitution, which provides a stricter standard of protection than Article 49 of the Charter. As already explained, the reference led the Court to overrule *Taricco* in part, avoiding a constitutional conflict, but the legal reasoning justifying that position was not completely clear. The Court of Justice may reduce such risks by consistently adopting a high standard of protection, but it might not always be possible to adopt the highest standard. Even if it does, conflicts will not be excluded, since that choice may have consequences for less protective Member States or could harm other fundamental rights that receive increased protection in other states.

Thirdly, the strict limits set by the Court on the application of more protective national fundamental rights seem to leave little room for that higher protection. The application of those national standards will probably compromise the integrity of Union law in many cases of partial determination. Those limits are not easy to justify in normative terms. Subject to such conditions, those rights no longer seem to be 'fundamental': they appear to be demoted to a lower rank. In such cases, it could perhaps be more appropriate to carry out a balancing exercise between the impact on the values protected by the national fundamental right at stake and the consequences this would have for the primacy, uniformity, and effectiveness of Union law, avoiding a formalistic analysis under which any effect on one element of that triad could exclude the application of the higher national standard. Perhaps this kind of reasoning could have been used to justify the Court's decision in the *M.A.S. and M.B.* case.

[43] For the judgment in *M.A.S. and M.B.*, see chapter 3, note 18; for the judgment in *Taricco*, see chapter 3, note 17.

Only time will tell whether the Court was right in allowing for a framed degree of variation of fundamental rights protection among the Member States, instead of maintaining mutually exclusive fields of application, however defined, for the Charter and national fundamental rights.

Finally, in the large area of partial determination the Court's approach interferes with the wider political significance of the Charter. Blurring the responsibility for identifying breaches of fundamental rights and for putting an end to them, this approach could undermine the political function of the Charter as a vector of identity and legitimacy for the Union.

The final aspect of *Fransson* that deserves attention is the solution adopted in that case. As already said, after claiming jurisdiction, the judgment of the Court was extremely thin on substance, and it sent the case back to the national court with general guidance on the Charter and on the possible application of national standards. This looks like an international 'human rights' approach, defining a minimum level of protection, recognizing a large margin of appreciation to the states, and failing to extract a robust normative limit from the Charter. Through this thin interpretation, the Charter comes close to the European Convention on Human Rights, and the specificity of the law of integration can be ignored. The risk of 'contamination' through close contact with the Convention system was the main theme of Opinion 2/13, which is analyzed in the following section.

5

The story of the relationship between European integration and the European Convention on Human Rights is an intriguing one. As discussed earlier, both supranational instruments were disjointed parts of the constitutional reconstruction of post-war Western Europe. Each subsystem pursued the legal and institutional framing of the European nation states in its particular way. The Communities did so through 'integration', initially in the economic sphere, creating common institutions and decision-making processes, establishing an autonomous legal order endowed with direct effect and primacy and connected with the national legal orders through the preliminary rulings procedure, and gradually expanding into many other fields. The Convention, by contrast, remained a specialized international instrument for the protection of fundamental rights, not inserted into national law. Its main supranational mechanism was the direct action granted to individuals for the protection of those rights before the Strasbourg Court, once they had tried all available internal remedies to no avail.

For decades both systems were largely successful in taming the states and formalizing their relations through the rule of law, superseding the previous state of affairs in Europe. At some point, however, they entered a serious institutional crisis with which they are still struggling. One could say that they have been victims of their own success. The inordinate enlargement of their membership, which has become very heterogeneous and sometimes problematic, has led to serious problems of enforcement, along with increasing mistrust and institutional overburden. On the other hand, the resurgence of nationalistic attitudes, with their quick reflection in legal and institutional practice, has led to pressure on the supranational traits of both systems, with the risk of undermining the degree of legal discipline that was achieved in the past.

Long before that, however, both systems were interlinked through a different kind of relationship. As we have seen, at an early stage the Community developed its own mechanism for the protection of fundamental rights as general principles. The main source of inspiration for those principles, besides national constitutional law and other international instruments, was the European Convention on Human Rights and the case law of the Strasbourg Court. A similarly close relationship is maintained with the Charter, for which the Convention stands as the baseline of protection.

Very early on, lawyers and politicians also considered the accession of the Community to the Convention system with two aims: giving Community law the catalogue of fundamental rights it still lacked at the time and establishing the same kind of external review as existed in the Member States. In 1994 the Council asked the Court of Justice whether the Community could accede to the Convention. To the surprise of many, in Opinion 2/94 the Court declared that such a constitutional step could not be envisaged without a specific legal basis, which meant that accession required a Treaty amendment.[44]

A legal basis was introduced by the Treaty of Lisbon, not just allowing for accession but actually obliging the Union to accede. At the same time, no deadline was set and Protocol No 8 to the Treaties laid down a number of conditions. First, accession had to respect 'the specific characteristics of the Union and Union law', including 'the mechanisms necessary to ensure that proceedings by non-Member States and individual applications are correctly addressed to Member States and/or the Union as appropriate'. Secondly, it should not affect 'the competences of the Union or the powers of its institutions' and 'the situation of the Member States in relation to the [Convention]'. Finally, accession should be compatible with Article 344 TFEU, according to which the Member States 'undertake not to submit a dispute concerning the interpretation or application of the Treaties to any method of settlement other than those provided for therein'.

In view of the stark differences between the supranational method of integration and the method followed by the Convention, and of the lingering tensions about the proper scopes of application of Union and national fundamental rights, subsequently compounded by the overlapping area created by *Fransson*, this mandate could seem paradoxical and almost self-defeating. Squaring this circle in a satisfactory manner required a great deal of legal craftsmanship and a clear understanding of the specificity of Union law. For the Union, the main challenge was to erect solid walls between both systems in order to avoid a Trojan horse scenario that could end up weakening integration.

The negotiations between the Union, represented by the Commission, and the other Contracting Parties, went on for almost three years, and resulted in a draft agreement for accession in 2013. Before submitting it for signature and ratification, the Commission dutifully requested from the Court of Justice an *ex ante* Opinion on whether it was compatible with the Union Treaties. Besides showing loyalty to the Court as the authoritative

[44] Opinion 2/94 of 28 March 1996 EU:C:1996:140.

interpreter of Union law, this was a prudent decision. Accession will be a step of fundamental importance and the Treaty made it conditional on a number of requirements. Basic considerations of legal certainty advised submitting the draft agreement to 'preventive' rather than to 'pathological medicine' that might have led to an *ex post* annulment, creating a difficult situation vis-à-vis the other Contracting Parties.

The request put the Court in the strong institutional position that is typical of *ex ante* review, allowing legal arguments to play to their fullest extent. In the framework of that procedure, prudential and political considerations have a more limited role than in *ex post* legality review, because the 'prescribed treatment' will be less 'invasive' than the annulment of the act. The difference becomes clear if one compares Opinion 2/13[45] with the judgment in *Pringle*,[46] in which the Court ruled *ex post* on the compatibility of the Treaty establishing the European Stability Mechanism with Union law. That judgment could give the impression that the Court was adjudicating under so much pressure, fearing that a negative decision could have fatal consequences for the economic crisis, the single currency, and integration at large, that it had little choice but to uphold the legality of that Treaty while introducing a number of safeguards for the future, thus containing the damage as far as it could. By contrast, in Opinion 2/13 the Court was able to ground its decision on a robust restatement of the specificity of Union law, as it had done in the early 90s with the comparable Opinion 1/91.[47] Indeed, one could have the impression that in Opinion 2/13 the Court stated and did some things in defence of the integrity of Union law that it repressed in *Pringle*.

The repressed came back with unusual force. After presenting a faithful and, in these troubled times, courageous account of the main elements of the law of integration as the framework for its analysis, the Court carried out a detailed examination of the draft agreement, which it held to be incompatible with Union law on the basis of no less than seven objections.

[45] Opinion 2/13, *supra* note 1.
[46] Case C-370/12, *Pringle*, EU:C:2012:756 (on this decision, see chapter 7).
[47] Opinion 1/91 of the Court of 14 December 1991 (EU:C:1991:490).

The first objection refers to Article 53 of the Charter, interpreted in *Fransson* and *Melloni* to mean that 'the application of national standards of protection of fundamental rights must not compromise the level of protection provided for by the Charter or the primacy, unity, and effectiveness of EU law'. Since Article 53 of the Convention allows the Contracting Parties to lay down higher standards, the Court requires that provision to be coordinated with the Charter 'so that the power granted to the Member States by Article 53 of the [European Convention of Human Rights] is limited—with respect to the rights of the Charter that correspond to those guaranteed by the [Convention]—to that which is necessary to ensure that the level of protection provided for by the Charter and the primacy, unity and effectiveness of [Union] law are not compromised'.[48]

The second objection concerns the principle of mutual trust, which, in the area of freedom, security, and justice, requires the Member States 'save in special circumstances, to consider all the other Member States to be complying with [Union] law and particularly with the fundamental rights recognised by [Union] law', and to refrain from checking whether they have complied. The draft agreement 'fails to take into consideration the fact that the Member States have, by reason of their membership of the [Union], accepted that relationships between them as regards matters covered by the transfer of powers from the Member States to the [Union], are governed by [Union] law to the exclusion, if [Union] law so requires, of any other law'. In the draft agreement, the Union and its Member States are also considered as full Contracting Parties in their reciprocal relations, even where they are exclusively governed by Union law. This might require the Member States 'to check that another Member State has observed fundamental rights, even though [Union] law imposes an obligation of mutual trust between those Member States'.[49] That would be incompatible with the autonomy of Union law.

[48] Opinion 2/13, *supra* note 1, at paras. 188 and 189. For *Fransson* and *Melloni*, see, respectively, chapter 5, note 75 and note 38 of this chapter.

[49] Opinion 2/13, *supra* note 1, at paras. 191–4.

The third objection relates to the preliminary rulings procedure. Protocol No 16 to the Convention allows the highest courts of the Contracting Parties to request the Strasbourg Court to give advisory opinions. This procedure could interfere with the obligation to refer preliminary questions under Article 267 TFEU, especially for Charter rights corresponding to Convention rights. The Court fears that the prior involvement procedure could be triggered in that context, circumventing the preliminary rulings procedure.

The fourth objection is based on Article 344 TFEU, according to which the Member States 'undertake not to submit a dispute concerning the interpretation or application of the Treaties to any method of settlement other than those provided for therein'. By contrast, Article 33 of the Convention allows for the resolution of disputes between Contracting Parties before the Strasbourg Court. For the Court this would also go 'against the very nature of [Union] law, which . . . requires that relations between the Member States be governed by [Union] law to the exclusion, if [Union] law so requires, of any other law'. In consequence, 'only the express exclusion of the [European Court of Human Rights'] jurisdiction under Article 33 of the [Convention] over disputes between Member States or between Member States and the [Union] in relation to the application of the [Convention] within the scope *ratione materiae* of [Union] law would be compatible with Article 344 TFEU'.[50]

The fifth objection refers to the 'co-respondent mechanism', which would allow the Union to become co-respondent in a case brought against one of its states, or vice-versa. The Union or its states may become 'co-respondents' either by a non-binding invitation of the Strasbourg Court or by a binding decision of that Court following a request from the Union or one or more Member States. In reviewing those requests, the Strasbourg Court 'would be required to assess the rules of [Union] law governing the division of powers between the [Union] and its Member States as well as the criteria for the attribution of their acts or omissions'. The same is true for the decisions of that Court

[50] *Ibid.*, at paras. 212 and 213.

on the apportionment of responsibility between the Union and its states for breaches of the Convention. Those decisions 'risk adversely affecting the division of powers between the [Union] and its Member States', impinging upon the exclusive jurisdiction of the Court.[51]

The sixth objection has to do with the procedure for the prior involvement of the Court of Justice in cases in which the Union is 'co-respondent' and on which that Court has not yet ruled. According to the draft agreement, the Strasbourg Court would be competent to decide whether the Luxembourg Court has already given a ruling, which would be 'tantamount to conferring on [the Strasbourg Court] jurisdiction to interpret the case law of the Court of Justice'. In addition, the procedure does not mention issues of interpretation of provisions of secondary law, which would allow the Strasbourg Court to interpret them on its own, in 'breach of the principle that the Court of Justice has exclusive jurisdiction over the definitive interpretation of [Union] law'.[52]

Finally, the Court objects to the conferral on the Strasbourg Court of a competence to review Union acts 'in the context of the [common foreign and security policy], and notably of those whose legality the Court of Justice cannot, for want of jurisdiction, review in the light of fundamental rights'. The review of those Union acts vis-à-vis the fundamental rights enshrined in the Convention would be entrusted 'exclusively to a non-[Union] body'. This, even though it is 'a consequence of the way in which the Court's powers are structured at present', 'fails to have regard to the specific characteristics of [Union] law'.[53]

The obvious consequence of these objections is that the Union cannot sign and ratify the draft agreement unless its provisions—or those of Union law with which it is incompatible—are amended. Serious rethinking and redrafting and a request for a second Opinion of the Court will be necessary before the Union can accede to the Convention with sufficient guarantees for the preservation of the integrity of its law.

[51] *Ibid.*, at paras. 224 and 231.
[52] *Ibid.*, at paras. 239 and 246.
[53] *Ibid.*, at paras. 254, 255 and 257.

Opinion 2/13 has attracted widespread and harsh criticism,[54] with very few voices coming out in its defence, and even those generally only in part.[55] The prevailing view is that the Court's staunch defence of the autonomy of Union law is a mere pretext, since the draft agreement would not put it at risk or, in any event, a positive Opinion subject to some interpretative caveats, as suggested by Advocate General Kokott,[56] would have been sufficient. The excessive zeal of the Court's Opinion could reveal a hidden agenda. The Court could be defending its own institutional position, not wanting to be subject to direct review by the Strasbourg Court. This has unfortunate substantive consequences that are not just temporary, because an easy and quick fix to the objections raised by the Court is not feasible. For the foreseeable future the Union will not be subject to the external fundamental rights review required by primary law. In this view, the Opinion thus reflects a distorted reading of the Treaty, all but ignoring that the Union is bound and not simply empowered to access the Convention.

This critique is a serious blow to the credit of the Court as a principled institution committed to the rule of law. Before dismissing the Opinion as an example of institutional opportunism, however, we might want to take it a bit more seriously.

There is no doubt that, in its obsessive prolixity, Opinion 2/13 reflects an institutional anxiety. If there is such a thing as 'institutional character', the reader has the impression of a 'control freak' who wants to avoid every possible risk, small as it might be, and who wishes to leave nothing to chance or to the behaviour of other actors. This anxiety reflects a mistrust vis-à-vis those actors. What one needs to assess is whether that anxiety is just a strategy to avoid or at least delay being subject to the

[54] See, e.g., Eeckhout, 'Opinion 2/13 on EU Accession to the ECHR and Judicial Dialogue: Autonomy or Autarky', 48(4) *Fordham International Law Journal* (2015) 955; Martín y Pérez de Nanclares, 'El TJUE pierde el rumbo en el dictamen 2/13: ¿Merece todavía la pena la adhesión de la UE al CEDH?', 52 *Revista de Derecho Comunitario Europeo* (2015) 825.

[55] See Halberstam, '"It's the Autonomy, Stupid!" A Modest Defence of Opinion 2/13 on EU Accession to the ECHR, and the Way Forward', 16(1) *German Law Journal* (2015) 105.

[56] View of 13 June 2014, EU:C:2014:2475.

oversight of the Strasbourg Court, or whether it is a legitimate existential angst due to a risk of irretrievable damage to the specificity of the Union system, and to the central role of the Court in that system.

A formal clash and a potential risk are hard to deny as regards Article 344 TFEU. Protocol No 8 to the Union Treaties required accession not to affect that provision. By contrast, the draft agreement did not exclude the use of the procedure of Article 33 of the Convention by the Union and its states to settle disputes relating to Union law in a forum other than the Court of Justice. Although in both systems the likelihood of those disputes is limited, they are not hypothetical.[57] This objection is similar to the one based on the principle of mutual trust, which also claims that within the scope of Union law relations between the Member States are exclusively governed by that law.

The deeper meaning of these objections, where the Court seems to be saying what it felt it could not say so clearly in *Pringle*, concerns the nature of integration, which is a process that permanently changes the status of the Member States. In the fields covered by Union law, and unless Union law itself authorizes it, those states may no longer entertain relations among themselves pursuant to international law. Here and elsewhere, the Opinion underlines the priority of integration over other forms of cooperation. The Court of Justice does not see Union law as one among the various methods of cooperation that could be open to the Member States. Those states are bound to use Union law when they want to cooperate in matters covered by it, and they must also respect its specificity when they are entitled to engage in international relations among themselves.

Similar concerns for the autonomy of Union law seem clear in respect of the issues relating to the advisory and prior involvement procedures and the co-respondent mechanism. The absence of limits to the use of those procedures when

[57] See, e.g., Case C-388/95, *Belgium v. Spain*, EU:C:2000:244 and ECtHR, *Slovenia v. Croatia*, Appl. no. 54155/16 (press release ECHR 340(2016) of 20 October 2016). On the interpretation of Article 344 TFEU, see Case C-459/03, *Commission v. Ireland*, EU:C:2006:345.

Union law is at stake entails potential dangers for the integrity of that law, as the Strasbourg Court could take decisions on issues relating to the division of powers between the Member States and the Union, on the interpretation of the case law of the Court of Justice, or be seized in a procedural context in which the preliminary rulings procedure has been circumvented.

The Court's concerns also seem to be warranted as regards the conferral to the Strasbourg Court of a competence to review Union acts adopted in the framework of the common foreign and security policy, where the Court has a very limited competence. It is not convincing to argue that the drafters of the Treaty of Lisbon knew that the Court's jurisdiction was limited and nonetheless required accession. First, it would be more reasonable to consider that accession had to be limited to the extent to which the Court could exercise its jurisdiction in that field, i.e. to the issue of individual sanctions. Secondly, in that section of the Opinion the Court does not follow a flat interpretation of the Treaties, in which all primary law provisions, be they in the Treaties or in Protocols, have exactly the same legal value. For the Court, some primary law provisions and principles have more weight than others and guide the interpretation of those other provisions. It is this 'stratified' approach to primary law, already visible in Opinion 1/91,[58] which leads the Court to consider that the attribution of a competence to an external court to review Union acts, while the Union Courts themselves are incompetent (unlike the courts of other contracting parties), is incompatible with the system of integration. This is the thorniest objection made by the Opinion, as solving it would require a modification of the Union Treaties, or else to limit the competence of the Strasbourg Court to the review of those decisions which also fall under the competence of the Court of Justice.

From these objections one may deduce two things. The first is that the source of the Court's mistrust is not the Strasbourg Court. The Court would not object to coming under its jurisdiction if proper conditions were in place. The Court's institutional

[58] Opinion 1/91, *supra* note 47. For another recent example of a 'stratified' interpretation of the Treaty, see the judgment in *Rosneft*, see chapter 4, note 35.

anxiety and mistrust seems, rather, to relate to the Member States of the Union. The draft agreement is perceived by the Court as a Trojan horse built by those states—a vehicle that could be used to dilute the discipline of integration, or to reduce the Charter to a replica of the Convention. This explains the Court's insistence on the need for solid institutional and normative walls between the systems, to avoid any contamination, and its insistence on the fact that the relevant actor for accession is the Union and that relations between the Member States are exclusively governed by Union law. This could also explain the insistence on express and prior safeguards to be introduced in the draft agreement. Unilateral declarations, such as those suggested by Advocate General Kokott to pave the way for a quick accession, or placing trust in the willingness of the Member States to respect Union law, are not enough for the Court—and perhaps rightly so. Once the draft agreement was in force, the interpretation and application of those soft safeguards would have been entrusted to the Member States in a different legal order, subject to the jurisdiction of another judicial body, and there was a real risk that the solutions adopted within that other system could diverge from the requirements of Union law, thus undermining it as the normal framework of relations between those states.

In other parts of the Opinion, even though the aim of preserving the integrity of Union law seems genuine, the problems detected by the Court are due to the objective difficulty in tracing the dividing line between Union law and state law and in apportioning responsibility for breaches of fundamental rights. The 'hybrid' area traced by the Court in *Fransson* may have exacerbated those problems. A clearer line dividing those spheres could solve some of the difficulties identified by the Court, as the Union would be the only relevant party for accession, which would only concern the scope of Union law. Thus, for example, Article 53 of the Convention would only allow the Union (not its Member States), in cases falling under the scope of Union law, to lay down higher standards as a matter of that law. Similarly, the higher court of the contracting party which could request an advisory opinion from the Strasbourg Court could only be the Court of Justice, not the higher courts of the Member States. And the border problems to be dealt with by the co-respondent mechanism would be limited to those few cases in which the interference with a fundamental right was really due to the joint and indiscernible action of the Union and its Member States.

That simpler solution may not be feasible. In view of the grounds for the Court's position in *Fransson* and *Melloni*, and of its clear advantages, it is not likely that a neat dividing line will be traced at all, be it for the internal purposes of the Union legal order or for the Union's accession to the Convention. The hybrid area of 'partial determination' carries with it, however, intractable problems of articulation with the Convention system.

6

From an initial position in which fundamental rights were almost absent from the Treaties, we have reached a situation in which there are so many sources, references and cross-references that their protection has become a daunting task. This complexity is reflected in the confusing instructions contained in the horizontal provisions of the Charter, which seem to challenge the interpreter to square a normative circle, and in the solution adopted in *Fransson* and *Melloni* for cases of 'partial determination'. The system will become even more complex when the Union accedes to the European Convention on Human Rights.

And yet, when compared to the human rights situation in less privileged parts of the world, fundamental rights protection in the Union seems to be largely satisfactory. One may therefore wonder about the reasons for this multiplication of sources and for the problematic character of these issues in the Union system.

This normative noise and excess, and the confusion and tensions surrounding it, may be a symptom of its legitimacy gap, whether perceived or real, and of the political malaise and institutional crisis in contemporary Europe.

The widespread perception according to which the democratic credentials of the Union are defective might be the main reason for this profusion, as it could be considered that such problems may be assuaged, if not totally resolved, through fundamental rights.[59] In this context, the Charter of Fundamental Rights seeks to give more visibility to Union fundamental rights, to promote a European identity around shared values, and to increase legitimacy. It is doubtful, however, that those objectives can be achieved, in view of increased legal complexity, problems of enforcement, and thin or inconclusive interpretations by the Court, and in the absence of any significant improvement in the processes of representation and decision-making of the Union.

The reason for the confusion and tensions surrounding these issues is to be found in the ambivalent attitude of the Member States and of their legal orders vis-à-vis their shared supranational organization. The resistance to the protection of fundamental rights pursuant to Union law, within the scope defined by the latter, and in accordance to its own standards reveals, once again, a lack of memory about the ultimate aims of integration and a reassertion of the nation state as the predominant form of political organization in contemporary Europe.

[59] See my article 'What's Left of the Charter: Reflections on Law and Political Mythology', *Maastricht Journal of European and Comparative Law* (2008) 65.

7

RIGIDITY, FRAGMENTATION, AND THE ALLURE OF INTERNATIONAL LAW

1

Let us go back one last time to the image, evoked at the beginning of this book, of the system of integration as a 'mobile'—a sophisticated normative and institutional structure with an existence of its own, intended to be much more than a sum of disjointed parts, and endowed with sufficient resources to grow and develop, adapt to changes, find successive points of equilibrium, and cope with erosion and serious crises. This system has allowed Europe, which previously existed mostly as a territorial notion, when not as a battlefield, to become a political reality in its own right, binding and taming its states through law, within the framework of a common and more sustainable organization. Indeed, integration was meant to transform, deeply and permanently, the position and the very nature of those states. And for decades it has been rather successful in doing so, building a solid web of relations, shared interests, and normative ties among the Member States in the framework of their common creation.

Today, Pescatore's experience of satori in front of Calder's 'mobile' would perhaps turn into a scream of despair. The main lines of the original structure are still visible beneath subsequent developments, but the 'mobile' has become complex, rigid, and entangled. While many may consider that it still fulfils its main objectives and remains a positive asset for Europe at large, it cannot be denied that in some respects its functioning is far from satisfactory.

There are several reasons for this regression. The first reason, evoked in chapter 2, is the waning of the initial impulse embodied in the Schuman declaration, which became weakened and seemingly exhausted before the project of integration could be brought to a more perfect and stable form. A second reason is the inordinate widening of the Union, in territorial and also in substantive terms, which took place without properly preparing the system for it, and which has led to a degree of malfunctioning and also to a setback in the level of trust between increasingly heterogeneous Member States. A third reason, compounding the other two, is the overall climate of economic and political crisis, with negative effects for the weakest elements of integration, unable to react properly as a result of defects in their design.

The decline prompted by these elements has become pervasive and undermines the legitimacy of the Union. At present it seems to affect, to varying degrees, the whole edifice of integration, including its most robust and established parts. The virtuous and elegant 'mobile' of the early decades looks more and more like a defective machine that, rather than searching for a new lasting balance, continuously produces its own misbalance. Its institutional and legal resources seem unable to cope with the current crisis. Its discipline is widely perceived as a straitjacket to be untied in order to allow the Member States to regain the lost paradise of unbound sovereignty. Some are tempted to roll-back integration or to abandon it for good, dismissing its supposedly naïve premises and its technocratic rationality, and burying it with other unfinished projects of modernity before returning to a more or less assertive nationalism.

In this unprecedented climate of decay, in comparison to which all the previous crises, including the 'empty chair' crisis, seem quite trite, the very idea of integration is shattered to its bones. The Member States no longer seem to agree on a basic shared understanding of integration. Different groups of states appear to have incompatible views about what the Union and Union law are, and about the consequences of being a Member State. This creates very difficult conditions for the subsistence of integration as we knew it, and for the practice of its law. This is not limited to the United Kingdom, with its traditional scepticism and now on its way to withdraw from the Union. It seems likely that the Member States and peoples that remain genuinely committed to the original design and ambitions of integration are not many, and that essential and powerful states, who owe part of what they have become to the European project, have an ambivalent attitude towards its basic tenets, and would sometimes prefer to interact in a softer framework of cooperation.

This endangers the viability of integration. If a basic overlapping consensus regarding the nature, scope, and purpose of the Union and its law ceases to exist among the Member States and their peoples, the conditions required for further integration, and even for maintaining the level of integration achieved so far, may be lacking. The absence of a shared understanding threatens to transform the Union into what it was never meant to be: the mere sum of its disjointed parts, an amorphous mass of polities and policies, without an autonomous existence, unable to foster the European general interest in any meaningful way. In this situation, Europe could become, once again, a purely territorial notion, if not a battlefield for power struggles—no longer an integrated and ordered space but a suboptimal area of policies that do not satisfy anybody.

This would lead to the failure of integration, which would appear as a thin patina with no substance of its own. The states would not have been deeply and permanently transformed through it, but simply reconstructed and strengthened. Through these decades the nation state would have remained the main locus of power, legitimacy, and law. And once the reconstruction had been completed, the Union would have to be restructured.

Since law has been and remains the privileged vehicle of integration and its most developed supranational element, it is only normal that the existing centrifugal forces put pressure on it in various ways, including pressure on the Court, the institution that, in its role as authoritative interpreter of the Treaties, remains the key preservationist actor of the system. Case law, however, is only one of the channels through which change—and resistance to change—takes place in the Union, and its actual significance can only be grasped once its relationship with other mechanisms is understood.

2

The formal mechanism for constitutional change in the Union is the procedure for the revision of the Treaties.[1] If primary

[1] On this subject, see my previous reflections in 'Between Unanimity and Utopia: Constitutional Change in the Union', in J. Baquero Cruz and C. Closa

law had to be adapted to new circumstances, that would be the natural method by which to do so. However, that procedure has become extremely inefficient for three interrelated reasons.

First, through the decades the mass of primary law has grown exponentially, with an extraordinary accumulation of legal provisions at a level of technical detail that seems improper for a fundamental text. This affects the whole body of primary law but it is more visible in certain parts, such as the provisions on economic and monetary union or some of the protocols to the Treaties. The European Convention failed in its attempt at simplifying primary law, which was one of its central tasks, in the Treaty establishing a Constitution for Europe. The Treaty of Lisbon simply followed that model and did not tackle the problem.

Secondly, the rigid rule governing Treaty change, requiring a unanimous agreement in an intergovernmental conference that must be ratified by all the Member States, became ever more rigid with each successive enlargement of the Union. The exponential multiplication of membership has altered the meaning and implications of the rule so much that the change leaps from quality to quantity. A unanimous agreement to be ratified among the initial, more homogeneous group, of six Member States has little in common with the current requirement of a unanimous agreement and ratification among 28 very different Member States. In numerical terms, the original veto position represented 17 per cent of the membership, while at present it amounts to a mere 3.6 per cent.

Thirdly, while primary law was becoming saturated, the European Convention and its aftermath failed to improve significantly the rigid rule on Treaty revision. The new '*simplified* revision procedure', which only applies to certain provisions of primary law and cannot be used to increase the competences of the Union, is only slightly less cumbersome than the ordinary revision procedure. The main difference is that in the former the

Montero (eds.), *European Integration from Rome to Berlin: 1957–2007* (2009), at 211–28.

unanimous decision to be ratified by all the Member States is adopted by the European Council and not by an intergovernmental conference. To change primary law one always needs to obtain a unanimous agreement and to have it ratified in all the Member States.

At present, therefore, amending the Treaties has become a heroic and almost desperate enterprise, if it is feasible at all. The agreement reached by the executives of the Member States will always be suboptimal, a result of hard bargaining and little deliberation among strong veto positions, not really useful to improve the constitutional framework of the Union in the general interest of its citizens. Whatever the outcome of the negotiations, few Member States, if any, will be happy about it. Besides, many of the agreed provisions will be highly ambiguous and there will be many 'leftovers' for the future. Finally, there is a high risk that even that sorry compromise might not be ratified because of a mishap, here or there, in a long and difficult ratification process.

The incapacity or unwillingness to slim down the mass of primary law, and to rethink the Treaty revision procedure in any meaningful way while the growing membership was rendering it highly dysfunctional, is the gravest constitutional failure of integration, and has led to many other problems by preventing the system from being adapted to changing circumstances. This omission is not to be found only in the failure to rethink the spirit of the revision procedure. It also lies in the inability to recreate among the 12, the 15, and the 28 a framework for constitutional revision that would be functionally equivalent to the one originally conceived for the six founding Member States.

This incapacity reflects the waning of the initial drive behind integration, the growing mistrust between the states, and the obsessive quest for intergovernmental control—which is, in point of fact, no more than an illusion of control, but one with very real negative consequences for the adaptability of the fundamental structures of the system. This failure may also explain the recurrent processes of Treaty revision from the Single European Act to the Treaty of Lisbon: an endless series of amendments that could never allow the Union to overcome its deficiencies and to be able to cope with the pressing contemporary challenges of integration.[2]

At the same time, paradoxically, these extremely rigid rules of change tend to protect the achievements of integration vis-à-vis the current pull towards intergovernmental control and disintegration, as a single state genuinely committed to integration can effectively block that drive, especially if it is a powerful one. As suggested in chapter 2, however, that protection may be excessive, impairing a positive evolution and resulting in unacceptable decision-making costs.

The solution to this dysfunctional element of the Union system is as easy to conceive as it is difficult to put into practice, let alone to discuss. In spite of its fundamental importance, this theme constitutes a taboo in integration. If it could be approached in a more rational manner, the Member States could first streamline the Treaties, keeping only those provisions that are important enough to be maintained at the highest level of the legal system in the Treaties, and demoting the remainder to secondary law. As a second step, they could unanimously amend the Treaty revision rules, introducing a super-qualified majority that would allow for a more satisfactory process of constitutional change. They could even consider a two-layer structure for primary law, with a supra-constitutional level, subject to more stringent rules if it is to be changed, and a level of 'ordinary' constitutionality, subject to less rigid rules. This evolution remains unthinkable in the present situation of mistrust and blind belief in the illusory protection offered by the existing procedure.

A reduction of the Union to a more cohesive group of Member States could facilitate evolution of the rules of change among them, but it is not clear that even that group, if it kept the commitment to the initial aims and tenets of integration, would be able to understand that the adoption of less rigid rules for the revision of primary law would be beneficial to all members.

[2] See B. de Witte, 'The Semi-Permanent Treaty Revision Process', in P. Beaumont and others (eds.), *Convergence and Divergence in European Public Law* (2002) 39.

A possible reduction in the Union's membership should not be seen as a catastrophic event to be avoided at all costs, or as another taboo. It cannot be denied that the Union is already broken up in various ways, from within, between north and south, centre and periphery, rich and poor, 'ins' and 'outs' in various key policies, and more fundamentally between groups of states for whom the very idea of the Union and the consequences of belonging to it seem incompatible.

As I have already suggested, besides creating very difficult conditions for political and legal practice, this situation might lead the Union to a graver catastrophe of implosion, or to a state of paralysis due to its inherent contradictions. Unity is an essential value of the Union, but it cannot override other equally important values. In particular, it should not override the value of integration—its depth, its intensity, and its commitment to a shared rule of law and to common institutions. There is a trade-off between widening and deepening, and a breaking point at which keeping the unity of the Union, valuable as it is, weighs less than the achievements of integration.

If and when that breaking point is reached, perhaps it would be preferable to take note of the inner division, reducing the formal membership of the Union to a core group of states sharing compatible values and views about integration, while keeping the remainder states in another circle, linked to the core through softer forms of economic cooperation such as those of the European Economic Area. Perhaps that core group of Member States could then agree to modify the Treaties through a less dysfunctional procedure. Perhaps, finally, it would form a smaller and more coherent Union, possibly less powerful in political and economic terms, but one that could promote fairer and more effective policies between its states and peoples.

Before changes of such magnitude—a sort of fundamental reset of the system—are possible, if they are ever considered, the existing system needs to cope with unprecedented pressure, and it is striving to avoid implosion through various other means. It is in the assessment of those means that a 'stress test' of the Union should be carried out and the state of health of integration assessed.

3

The first mechanism used to adapt the rigid and dense rules of primary law to new circumstances while leaving their wording intact is judicial interpretation. This mechanism has traditionally played a key role in the development of integration, but the conditions under which it operates at present are rather different.

In any event, the possibilities of constitutional mutation without treaty change are not without limits. First of all, this method can be used within the margins of acceptable judicial interpretation, but it cannot go against the explicit wording of a provision. Although the actual boundary between interpretation and revision is more difficult to trace than some might think, certain changes clearly require a modification of the wording of treaty provisions. Secondly, the interpretation of the multilingual texts of Union primary law may have become less flexible as regards recently adopted treaty provisions. The earlier case law, freed from original interpretation in the absence of the *travaux préparatoires*, which remained secret, focused on *telos* and context as the decisive elements used to find the meaning of the complex multilingual text. By contrast, original interpretation sometimes plays a greater and even decisive role as regards more recent Treaty provisions, in view of the abundance of materials regarding their genesis and the intention of their drafters.[3] Besides the massive political pressure exerted on the Court in sensitive cases, there is, objectively, less space for the creativity of the Court. The interpretation of older provisions is already determined by a mass of precedents. That of more recent provisions is often rigidified by a wealth of information about authorial intent.

It is important to note, thirdly, that the normative weight of judgments interpreting the Treaties is directly connected to the difficulty of amending them. If revising primary law is very difficult, and in some cases close to impossible, then the case law of the Court interpreting that law becomes very entrenched. With the spectacular enlargement of the Union, it is now almost

[3] See, among other examples, *Fransson*, chapter 5, note 75, and Case C-583/11 P, *Inuit*, EU:C:2013:625.

impossible to revert the case law of the Court interpreting primary law through Treaty revisions. This possibility, it should be recalled, has almost never been used, and was never used in the foundational period, when the six founding states could have more easily done so. At least in theory, nevertheless, the current extreme constitutional rigidity entails an increased responsibility for the Court in its interpretations. On the one hand, the Court may feel that some decisions are not for it to take, in view of their far-reaching consequences, but should be left for the organs entrusted with the revision of the Treaties. On the other hand, very often it will be risky to leave the burden of constitutional adaptation to those organs, as the Treaty revision procedure may produce no change or only marginal changes. Constitutional rigidity also entails a higher pressure on the Court to modify its case law, whether explicitly or implicitly, to pave the way for changes that would be impossible to obtain through Treaty or legislative amendments. Those changes can also be restrictive, prompted by the centrifugal forces at play in integration and leading to sacrifices of bits and pieces of the *acquis*.

The preceding chapters have tried to explain and assess, mostly through an analysis of recent important judgments, how the Court is reacting to that kind of pressure. One could wonder whether there is a logic behind the chain of reactions, or whether they depend on random factors such as the composition of the Grand Chamber when deciding each case. At first sight, the picture could seem perplexing. While *Dano*[4] retreats from prior integrationist case law as regards the substance of the citizenship rights for a particularly vulnerable category of persons, *Fransson*[5] confirms settled case law concerning the scope of application of Union fundamental rights, while conceding a limited possibility for the parallel application of national fundamental rights in cases of 'partial determination'. Although the most ambivalent case, *Pringle*,[6] to be discussed later, accepts a development of dubious consequences for the integrity of Union law while voicing certain safeguards, and *M.A.S. and M.B.* partly

[4] *Dano*, see chapter 5, note 53. [5] *Fransson*, see chapter 5, note 75.
[6] *Pringle*, see chapter 6, note 46.

overrules *Taricco* and admits the temporary application of the higher national protection of a fundamental right which compromises the Union's financial interests, Opinion 2/13 and *Achmea* put forward a vigorous and orthodox defence of the law of integration with regard, respectively, to the various risks of dilution lurking behind the envisaged accession to the European Convention on Human Rights, and to the phenomenon of bilateral investment treaties between Member States.[7] And in *Gauweiler*[8] the Court also resisted pressure from the German Constitutional Court, adopting a reasonably flexible reading of the powers of the European Central Bank and protecting the European general interest.

While the analysis presented in this book was limited to certain leading judgments, it seems to me that it could be generalized, as comparable pressures and reactions are present throughout the system, to a variety of degrees. If such a generalization is justified, the overall picture of the Court's reaction would combine a robust defence of the structural elements of the system coupled with limited concessions regarding some substantive aspects. In most cases, the Court is behaving as a principled institution, protecting the key elements of the law of integration while 'sacrificing' some pieces of the substantive *acquis*—which it could perhaps reclaim later.

This would mean that the present centrifugal forces cannot count on the Court to follow their views towards dismantling the *acquis* and could at most obtain some 'compensating' victories here and there. On the other hand, the preservationist forces at play in the Union can count on the Court to protect the main structural elements of integration and many of its substantive achievements. The overall result could be that the centrifugal forces, while trying their chance at the Court in this or that case, will not concentrate their activity in the judicial process, from which they cannot expect a general reversal of integration, and will deploy most of their efforts in the political process.

[7] For Opinion 2/13, see chapter 6, note 1; Case C-284/16, *Achmea*, EU:C:2018:158.

[8] *Gauweiler*, chapter 3, note 11.

4

A second instrument that allows the Union to deal with its present situation can be found in the various phenomena of asymmetric integration accepted by the Union system. The differing views on the nature of the Union and on the meaning of being a Member State are not overcome through these mechanisms, but they are alleviated because a group of Member States is allowed to move ahead with particular policy measures while other Member States do not participate in them. Strong disagreements about the nature of the Union may remain in place, but there is agreement that in some policy areas being a Member State does not always entail the same consequences.

Asymmetric integration may take the form of primary law exclusions from specific policy areas (economic and monetary union, Schengen),[9] which could be of a permanent or temporary nature, and with or without the possibility of opting in. It may also take the form of measures of secondary law adopted pursuant to enhanced cooperation. Before the entry into force of the Treaty of Lisbon this possibility had never been used, but now there are several examples of such measures.[10] Whatever the form, we are witnessing an increasing use of that type of measure, with the ensuing fragmentation of the Union, in policy and legal terms—a fragmentation that sits uncomfortably with the very idea of 'integration' and creates complex conditions for the integrity of Union law.

[9] See Protocols No 15 to 17, 19, 21, and 22 to the Treaties.

[10] See Council Regulation 1259/2010 implementing enhanced cooperation in the area of the law applicable to divorce and legal separation, OJ 2010 L 343/10; European Parliament and Council Regulation 1257/2012 implementing enhanced cooperation in the area of the creation of unitary patent protection, OJ 2012 L 361/1; Council Regulation 2016/1104 implementing enhanced cooperation in the area of jurisdiction, applicable law and the recognition and enforcement of decisions in matters of the property consequences of registered partnerships, OJ 2016 L 183/30; Council Regulation 2016/1103 implementing enhanced cooperation in the area of jurisdiction, applicable law and the recognition and enforcement of decisions in matters of matrimonial property regimes, OJ 2016 L 183/1; and Council Regulation 2017/1939 implementing enhanced cooperation on the establishment of the European Public Prosecutor's Office, OJ 2017 L 283/1.

This fragmentation, however, is part of the system as it has evolved in recent years, and one should try to understand its multiple causes, its meaning in historical perspective, and its possible consequences for the future. In addition, a jurist should try to determine whether and to what extent these phenomena are compatible with Union law.

The first thing to note is that asymmetric integration should not be equated with disintegration and also that, in this context, an insistence in preserving 'unity' at all costs is misconceived. Asymmetric integration is an ambivalent phenomenon. It represents a process of further integration among a group of Member States, while other states do not engage in it. A key objective of integration, that of establishing interdependence and solidarity among all the Member States, is sacrificed. Asymmetric integration may alleviate the cleavages between groups of Member States, but it also renders them visible.

When it is directly provided for at the level of primary law, which may allow a group of Member States to pursue a policy among themselves, asymmetric integration may be seen an escape valve from the rigidity of the Treaty revision procedure. This is the case for both economic and monetary union and Schengen, through different techniques. Since this is done through primary law, Union law cannot object to it, but these phenomena should not endanger the fundamental principles of the Union legal order, such as the institutional balance, the principle of sincere cooperation among the Member States, or provisions of the Treaty that bind all those states. Beyond that, the fragmentation due to these forms of asymmetric integration in primary law is not legally objectionable, as it takes place within the system.

Secondly, as regards fragmentation in secondary law through enhanced cooperation, the Union Treaties impose strict conditions and procedures for its use, which aim to ensure that those measures foster integration instead of undermining it. If and insofar as those conditions are respected, it can be presumed that the basic principles of integration are complied with.

In legal terms, therefore, these phenomena are acceptable in principle, as they are internal to the system and limited by principles and rules that bind all the Member States. Whether these phenomena are sustainable in political and institutional terms is a different and more pressing matter. It cannot be denied that they interfere with the institutional setting and with normal decision-making procedures, potentially eroding the overall political process of the Union and the unity of its institutional framework. If they became pervasive, at some point they could make the Union too fragmented and inconsistent, and this may damage the spirit of commonality of integration. Finally, if they always concern the same division among two or more groups of Member States, they could trace an inner circle, a Union within the Union—which may already be visible in some areas—a development that could harm the identity, legitimacy, and sustainability of the European project as a whole.

5

Another response to pressure is the trend to have recourse to international agreements between groups of Member States as a form of cooperation outside the Union framework, but closely connected to Union policies. There are several examples, initially in the staggered response to the sovereign debt crisis, with the European Stability Mechanism and the Fiscal Compact,[11] and thereafter with regard to measures closely related to the internal market, such as the European patent system and the single resolution mechanism, where excised Union legislation is completed by international agreements among most but not all Member States.[12] And we also had an international agreement

[11] Treaty establishing the European Stability Mechanism (between the States of the euro area), of 2 February 2012; Treaty on Stability, Coordination and Governance of the Economic and Monetary Union (between the States of the euro area and six other Member States for some parts; the Czech Republic, the United Kingdom and Croatia do not participate), of 2 March 2012.

[12] Regulation 1257/2012, on the creation of unitary patent protection, *supra* note 10, completed by the agreement on a Unified Patent Court (between 25 Member States), of 19 February 2013, OJ 2013 C 175/1; European Parliament and Council Regulation 806/2014 establishing uniform rules and a uniform procedure for the resolution of credit institutions and certain investment firms in the framework of the Single Resolution Mechanism and a Single Resolution Fund, OJ 2014 L 225/1, completed by the agreement on the transfer

in simplified form between *all* the Member States, also purportedly outside the Union legal order—the 'new settlement for the United Kingdom within the European Union'[13]—now defunct after the 'leave' result of the Brexit referendum.

In the past, international agreements in simplified form concluded by the Member States in the margins of the Council were sometimes used in areas in which the Treaties did not grant any competence, whether exclusive or shared, and were seen as complementing the law of integration.[14] At present, the competences of the Union are large enough, but the Member States seem to have rediscovered that practice and use it with increasing levity, also in areas that fall within the objectives and powers of the Union. Through this, they appear to regain part of their lost sovereignty or at least a measure of autonomy. This phenomenon, formally external to the system, is complex and highly problematic in legal and institutional terms. The key question is whether it is lawful and under what conditions. We also need to understand the reasons for this tendency and to assess its systemic effects on integration.

The main locus for such an assessment is the *Pringle* judgment, read in the light of Opinion 2/13,[15] but we first need to recall the traditional tensions between the law of integration and public international law.

As suggested in chapter 2, one of the central aims of integration was to overcome the structural deficiencies of international law by creating an institutional and legal system that would effectively bind the Member States into a common and autonomous discipline. The law of integration is, however, not antithetical to international law. It may be seen as an 'adaptive' evolution thereof, in the development of its political and legal architecture. It is, in a way, what international law could become

and mutualisation of contributions to the Single Resolution Fund (between 26 Member States), of 21 May 2014.

[13] See chapter 5, note 80.

[14] See Pescatore, 'Remarques sur la nature juridique des "décisions des représentants des États membres réunis au sin du Conseil"', *Sociaal-economische Wetgeving* (1966) 579.

[15] See chapter 6, note 1. See also *Achmea*, *supra* note 7, paras. 32–7.

if its subjects, the sovereign states, decided to make it more effective. And it comes close, on the other side of the spectrum, to confederal and federal entities. This is what makes the Union a *sui generis* system, torn between categories and models, and best understood in the specificity of its structure and functions.[16] This is, also, what brings to the fore the dogmatic issue of statehood—as the states rightly feel that integration limits their sovereignty.

Be it as it may, in symbolic and also in practical terms the law of integration needed to vindicate that specificity not only vis-à-vis national law but also with regard to international law, breaking the umbilical cord connecting it to the latter. This is a common theme of the jurisprudence of integration, with the statement that the Union is based on its own legal order, and also in the judgments in which the autonomous treaty-making power of the Union, as a subject of international law, is asserted.

For several decades, with some exceptions authorized by Union law itself (Articles 293 EC and 34(2)(d) EU), the law of integration was not just the preferred vehicle for relations between the Member States in the areas covered by it: it was an exclusive vehicle. Referring to those exceptions, Pierre Pescatore underlined that Community law was a 'legal universe of its own' ('*univers juridique à part*') in which the authors of the Treaties had preferred an institutional method for the adoption of secondary law, excluding the usual procedures of international law.[17] The issue of whether those states could go on entertaining parallel relations as a matter of international law, in fields covered by those Treaties and beyond the exceptions authorized by them, was not on the table for discussion for decades—for obvious reasons. Though it was occasionally used as a form of provisional closer cooperation between willing groups of states before those instruments were incorporated into Union law—for example with the Schengen and Prüm Treaties—the wider extension of Union competences, the introduction of enhanced cooperation with the Treaty of Amsterdam, and the deletion of Articles 293 EC and

[16] See Constantinesco, 'La spécificité du droit communautaire', *Revue trimestrielle du droit européen* (1966) 1.

[17] Pescatore, chapter 1, note 3, at 72.

34(2)(d) EU by the Treaty of Lisbon, made some consider that *inter se* agreements had been relegated 'to the footnotes of the European integration story'.[18]

From that perspective, it can clearly be seen that the current tendency of the Member States to do outside the Union framework things that they could arguably, and often clearly, do within that framework, is relevant not only or mainly in terms of fragmentation, but also as a device that could have fatal consequences for the integrity of Union law. Indeed, these phenomena could be seen as a form of flight from the discipline of integration, perceived as imposing excessive constraints on the Member States. The risk is that integration may be treated as an optional system that can gradually be emptied out or rolled back, no longer the exclusive vehicle for relations among the Member States in the areas falling within its scope.

This phenomenon is the most dangerous imaginable blow to the integrity of the Union as a polity and as a legal system, and the most powerful disintegrating device that could be used by the centrifugal forces at work within the system. Through it, the Union could seem to be walking back down the path of integration and reconstructing the umbilical cord connecting it to what many now see as the lost paradise to be regained: international law among sovereign nations, with its contingency and flexibility, and without the various 'discontents' of Union law.

Bruno de Witte has reviewed the possible causes of this phenomenon in the context of the sovereign debt crisis, finding that it responds to a 'complex series of reasons', among which he mentions the following: the limited budgetary resources of the Union; the qualms of some German constitutional lawyers about competence issues and about compliance with the no bail-out clause; the requirement for swift action and the wish to avoid the lengthy Union legislative process; and, for the fiscal compact, the German belief in the stronger symbolic message of an international agreement, and the need to circumvent the British veto allowed by the rigid Treaty amendment rules. For him, there is 'no evidence of a deliberate strategy

[18] B. de Witte, 'Using International Law in the Euro Crisis: Causes and Consequences', ARENA Working Paper 4/2013, at 2.

of the member state governments to assert "total control" of the economic governance reform process and to sideline the European Union institutions or marginalise the "Community method"'.[19]

This conclusion could seem surprising. All the alleged causes, except for the need to avoid the British veto to a Treaty amendment for what became the fiscal compact, seem to be contingent. Budgetary resources, to which some of these flights into international law are held to relate, could be supplemented if the political will to do so existed. Experience shows that a legislative procedure can also be concluded relatively quickly if there is a will to act within the Union framework. The alleged legal qualms about the no bail-out clause are due to an excessively restrictive reading of the Treaty, which was rejected by the Court.[20] The alleged symbolic value of an international agreement is not a credible argument, for international law has less force than Union law. Finally, the British veto to what became the fiscal compact could have easily been avoided, as de Witte himself concedes, through the adoption of an act of Union secondary law as an enhanced cooperation.[21]

The contingency of the reasons given for these international law excursions and the subsequent use of the same method of dissociation from the Union, going 'out' of it in cases for which the justification was even less convincing, suggest that something else is going on as a matter of law and politics.

It is hard not to perceive that the Member States, at least some of them and not those which are the least influential, currently have a highly ambivalent relation towards a Union that is their creation but which they see as something external to them, imposed on them, sometimes even curtailing them, and not wholly belonging to and controlled by them. In that context, the temptation to 'break free' from the discipline of integration and to recover a measure of autonomy, at least in sensitive areas, becomes very strong. The obvious explanation for these international agreements among groups of Member States, therefore, is that they wish or need to do some things together, but that

[19] *Ibid.*, at 3–9. [20] *Pringle*, see chapter 6, note 46, at paras. 130–47.
[21] de Witte, *supra* note 18, at 9.

they will only do them outside the Union framework. In some cases, the temptation to escape integration could be due to the rigidity of primary law, but in most cases the main reasons seem to be the reversibility of commitments in the sphere of international law, and the symbolic preservation of sovereignty.

For very sensitive measures, often involving significant financial resources in the context of a difficult and volatile crisis situation, it appears that some Member States thus prefer to act outside the Union framework, hoping to assert more influence and to be able to escape from their international law commitments and regain autonomy if anything goes wrong. The consequence is that the Union and its law are sidelined and weakened, although the institutions might be 'used' in one way or another.

6

The *Pringle* case was purely accidental. In normal circumstances, the Treaty establishing the European Stability Mechanism would have been concluded, ratified, and become operational without any involvement of the Court of Justice. Being a mechanism between all the Member States whose currency is the euro, litigation about it seemed unlikely. In addition, the limited role given to the Court by Article 37 of that Treaty only concerns its interpretation and application, not the legality of decisions taken pursuant to it. It was therefore a surprise that Mr Pringle, a member of the Irish Parliament, challenged its legality and also the validity of the European Council Decision amending Article 136 TFEU,[22] which supposedly paved the way for the establishment of the European Stability Mechanism, and that the Irish Supreme Court dutifully referred the case to the Court of Justice.

This gave the Court a chance to examine the legality of the amendment of Article 136 TFEU, assessing whether it could be adopted through a simplified revision procedure, and to provide

[22] European Council Decision 2011/199/EU, of 25 March 2011, amending Article 136 TFEU with regard to a stability mechanism for Member States whose currency is the euro, OJ 2011 L 91/1.

the national court with the elements of interpretation it needed to check the lawfulness of the European Stability Mechanism. More generally, the case allowed the Court to say something about the then still incipient selective flight of the Member States to international law. *Pringle* was, however, a mixed blessing. The economic stakes were so high that a negative decision was hardly conceivable, as it could have had far-reaching negative consequences for the European economy. As already suggested, the Court probably felt that it could not seriously consider questioning the legality of the Treaty amendment or of the international agreement between the Member States of the euro area. There seemed to be little space for law beneath the naked force of economic facts.

If the reasons for the unlawfulness of the simplified amendment of the Treaty and/or of the international agreement had been well founded, however, the Court could have considered a technique of adjudication that has been used in similar cases and that could be envisaged for other intractable cases that the future may bring: declaring the acts unlawful but maintaining their validity for the time required to find an adequate solution under Union law; or declaring the acts lawful for a provisional period of time during which the competent institutions should find a more orthodox solution. Nevertheless, the Court chose a different path, upholding the legality of the amendment of Article 136 TFEU, declaring that it was correctly adopted through the simplified procedure, and ruling that Union law did not preclude the Member States from entering into the Treaty establishing the European Stability Mechanism, while introducing a number of safeguards aimed at preserving the integrity of the Union system.

The approach of the Court may seem a significant concession to the centrifugal forces present in the Union system, giving its legal blessing to the disintegrative pull of international agreements between groups of Member States. On closer inspection, however, the *Pringle* judgment seems much more subtle and balanced.

On the one hand, the Court was bound to make two significant concessions to be able to uphold the legality of the amendment of Article 136 TFEU and of the *inter se* agreement. First of all, it states that the Union lacks *a specific competence* to establish the European Stability Mechanism. The judgment does so through a strict interpretation of Article 122(2) TFEU, not envisaging a contextual, systemic, or teleological reading of the provisions on economic and monetary union (whose *effet utile* and very rationality could seem to be compromised by the absence of such a competence), and avoiding any serious consideration of the notion of implied powers.

This restrictive reading could seem to entrench the defective constitutional design of economic and monetary union, giving the impression that it was created without the indispensable instruments to ensure its own survival in times of crisis. Indeed, a passage of the judgment suggests that the Union on its own would not be able to ensure 'the financial stability of the euro area as a whole', and that it is only through its involvement in that international mechanism that the Commission is enabled to promote 'the general interest of the Union'.[23]

In a second and closely related point, the Court interprets the new Article 136(3) TFEU as a purely declaratory provision that does not provide the legal basis for the mechanism, which is created through the Member States' own retained powers.[24] In other words, the Member States were doing something that they could have done in any event, even if the Union Treaties had not been amended. Article 136 TFEU simply confirmed this to ensure legal certainty, adding that this multilateral action in the sphere of international law has to be 'indispensable to safeguard the stability of the euro area as a whole' and 'subject to strict conditionality'.

These two concessions may seem risky, as they could lead the Member States to perceive the Union as a purely optional system lacking any effective closure. In fields falling outside the very limited exclusive competences of the Union set out in Article 3 TFEU and not pre-empted by the (reversible) exercise of shared competences, those states could use Union law as merely one among other possible frameworks for their cooperation. This is the view of Bruno de Witte, for whom 'the

[23] *Pringle*, see chapter 6, note 46, at para. 164.
[24] *Ibid.*, at paras. 68, 72, 73, 109, 184, and 185.

member states of the European Union are states, and therefore retain their capacity to conclude international treaties not only with third countries (which is the most frequent case) but also among each other, even when the subject matter of their agreement is closely connected to European Union matters'. Indeed, he considers that in areas outside the Union's exclusive competence '*inter se* agreements are permissible in principle'.[25]

This approach seems to consider that, outside exclusive and pre-empted shared competences, it would be indifferent for Union law whether the Member States act individually or collectively. If this approach were correct, the Member States could theoretically empty out the Union legal order of most of its content, repealing existing legislation falling under shared competence and readopting it outside the Union legal and institutional system, as international law, without amending the Treaties. The autonomy of Union law and its main *raison d'être* would be severely damaged by such a development, which would certainly please not only those jurists who consider international law as a useful tool for parallel cooperation among the Member States, but also those who see the nation state as the central political organization in contemporary Europe, and the Union as an obsolete organization to be downsized.

In the light of the safeguards contained in *Pringle* these views seem misguided. It is clear that as a matter of Union law, as interpreted by the Court, it is not indifferent whether the Member States exercise their retained competences individually or collectively—i.e. in a multilateral way that can compete and interfere with existing or future Union measures, pre-empting them. The opposite would be odd, as the main objective of integration is that of framing the interaction between the Member States in a common institutional and legal framework. A closer reading of *Pringle* shows that the international capacity retained by the Member States to conclude international agreements among themselves is much more limited than one might think at first sight. Moreover, that capacity is constrained by Union law to such an extent that it is misleading to compare it

[25] de Witte, *supra* note 18, at 2 and 16.

with the regular treaty-making power of sovereign nations not engaged in European integration.

As regards the scope of those retained powers, in four key passages of the judgment the Court mentions, as a condition for the lawfulness of the international agreement under review, that the Treaties do not confer any *specific power or competence* on the Union to establish a stability mechanism similar to the one envisaged by the Member States.[26] The insistence of the Court in this particular language reveals that this is an essential element of the balanced approach it followed. It is not only in cases in which *inter se* agreements concern the exclusive competences of the Union (such as monetary policy), or shared competences pre-empted by Union action, that the Member States would be precluded from concluding them. That would be an extremely weak defence of the integrity of the system, if it could count as a defence at all.

The Court's stance, based on the Union's order of competences and linked to the principle of sincere cooperation enshrined in Article 4(3) TEU, is much more robust.[27] The Member States are precluded from concluding *inter se* agreements in three situations: first, when those agreements concern exclusive competences of the Union set out in Article 3 TFEU; secondly, when they affect existing common rules or alter their scope;[28] and, finally, when the Treaty grants the Union *a specific competence* to do something, regardless of whether such a competence has already been used or not. In the third case, the Member States may act individually as long as the Union has not acted, but they may not enter into international agreements among themselves unless the Union authorizes it. In consequence, in areas falling under exclusive or specific competences, and in areas that are largely covered by existing primary or secondary Union law, the states are bound to use the Union framework if

[26] *Pringle*, see chapter 6, note 46, at paras. 64, 105, 168, and 180.

[27] In *Achmea*, *supra* note 7, para. 32, the Court recalled that international agreements, including those concluded between the Member States, 'cannot affect the allocation of powers fixed by the Treaties or, consequently, the autonomy of the EU legal system, observance of which is ensured by the Court'.

[28] *Pringle*, chapter 6, note 46, at paras. 98 and 101.

they want to act collectively with all the Member States—or with a group thereof establishing an enhanced cooperation.[29] To a large extent, therefore, the Court makes sure that the Union system will not become freely disposable.

This notion of 'specific power or competence' is clearly connected to Article 352 TFEU. We learn from the case law that that provision 'is designed to fill the gap where *no specific provisions* of the Treaty confer on the [Union] institutions express or implied powers to act, if such powers appear none the less to be necessary to enable the [Union] to carry out its functions with a view to attaining one of the objectives laid down by the Treaty'.[30] Legal bases other than Article 352 TFEU, such as, among various possible examples, Article 114 TFEU, should be considered as specific competences, and it would be in breach of Union law for the Member States to harmonize their legislations to ensure the proper functioning of the internal market—or to do any other thing for which the Treaties provide a specific power—through an *inter se* agreement.

Between exclusive and 'specific' competences and pre-empted areas of shared competence, and, on the other side of the spectrum, the complete absence of Union powers, where the Member States obviously retain their power to act collectively, the Court has opened an area of indeterminacy. The *Pringle* judgment does not state that a similar stability mechanism could not have been established pursuant to Union law. All the Court declares is that there was no *specific* legal basis to do so. The Court 'sacrifices' Article 352 TFEU, the general legal basis allowing the Council, acting unanimously and after having obtained the consent of the European Parliament, to adopt measures that are necessary to attain one of the objectives of the Treaties but for which they have provided no specific legal basis.

In paragraph 67 of the judgment the Court thus leaves open the question of whether the stability mechanism could be established on the basis of Article 352 TFEU and recalls that

[29] See Constantinesco, 'Les clauses de "cooperation renforcée"', *Revue trimestrielle de droit européen* (1997) 751.

[30] Opinion 2/94, chapter 6, note 44, at para. 29.

that provision 'does not impose on the Union any obligation to act'.[31]

Building on that aspect of the *Pringle* judgment, Article 352 TFEU is the legal basis of the draft Regulation by which the Commission has proposed to integrate the European Stability Mechanism, to be renamed the European Monetary Fund, into the Union system, while adding to it the function of providing the 'backstop' to the Single Resolution Fund.[32] Although the Court simply reserved its position on the question, the Commission proposal considers that that legal basis would be correct, as the main conditions for its use seem to be met: first, as confirmed by *Pringle*, there is no specific legal basis in the Treaties that could be used; secondly, the measure is indispensable to provide for stability in the euro area, an aim that squarely falls within the objectives of the Union in the light of Articles 3(3) and (4) TEU; finally, the integration of the mechanism into the Union system does not enlarge or modify the objectives of the Union, and cannot be seen as an irregular revision of the Treaties.

The concession of the Court regarding Article 352 TFEU may not be a big sacrifice, since that provision requires unanimity and its use has become marginal in contemporary Union legislative practice. Some could even think that the mechanism may be adopted more easily as an *inter se* agreement, avoiding the paralysing rigidity of unanimity among all the Member States under Article 352 TFEU, with the additional requirement of obtaining the approval of the German parliament before the competent German minister can cast a positive vote in the Council,[33] or the even more rigid Treaty revision procedure.

[31] *Ibid.*, at para. 67.

[32] Commission proposal for a Council Regulation on the establishment of the European Monetary Fund, COM(2017) 827, of 6 December 2017. For the Single Resolution Fund, see Regulation 806/2014, *supra* note 12.

[33] Judgment of the German Constitutional Court on the Lisbon Treaty, chapter 3, note 19, at para. 417: 'In so far as the flexibility clause under Article 352 TFEU is used, this always requires a law within the meaning of Article 23.1 second sentence of the Basic Law.' This requirement has been codified by the German legislature in Art. 8 of the *Integrationsverantwortungsgesetz* of 22 September 2009.

As a matter of fact, the Treaty establishing the European Stability Mechanism entered into force, in accordance with its Article 48, once it was ratified by contracting parties contributing 90 per cent of the funds. As far as its entry into force was concerned, this avoided the veto power of less willing Member States.

On the other hand, through this crack in the system the Court allows the Member States to alter profoundly some basic structures of integration. The main institutional traits of the European Stability Mechanism are its unanimous decision-making, even for individual decisions granting assistance to euro area Member States, with an emergency procedure that gives an individual veto power to three Member States; the absence of judicial review by the Court of Justice; the inapplicability of primary law and of the Charter, since the states are not acting within the scope of Union law;[34] the exclusion of the legislative procedure and of standard Union procedures for its implementation; and the lack of political accountability within the Union system. Such features modify the Union's institutional balance and seem rather dubious in terms of respect for the rule of law and democratic decision-making. Even though the European Stability Mechanism is framed and controlled, the phenomenon represents a real erosion of the system.

Beyond the system of competences, the *Pringle* judgment includes a second important safeguard. In the narrow space in which *inter se* agreements are possible, primacy deploys all its effects and the Court requires the Member States to comply with Union law.[35] The second part of the judgment indeed examines, in answer to the questions raised by the Irish Supreme Court, whether the international agreement is compatible with various provisions of Union law. Although that agreement is not formally part of Union law, through this device the Court embraces and frames *inter se* agreements, positing a relation of subordination between Union law and those instruments, and conceiving the latter as a sort of *sui generis* secondary law that must respect not only the Treaties or the constitutional essence of Union law, but Union law as a whole.

[34] *Pringle* judgment, see chapter 6, note 46, at para. 180.
[35] *Ibid.*, at paras. 69, 109, and 121.

The Treaty establishing the European Stability Mechanism among the Member States of the euro area is thus not at the same hierarchical level as the primary law on which the Union is founded. It may well be, in formal terms, an international agreement 'outside' the Union system, but it is connected to it in various ways. It may be asked where the source of that subordination lies, and why are such agreements not at the same level as primary law, with the consequences that would ensue from the Vienna Convention on the law of treaties. The reason is that they could hamper the autonomy of Union law and undermine the exclusive character of the procedure for the revision of the Union Treaties. This subordination clearly springs from the principles of primacy and of sincere cooperation. In the same way as with unilateral measures, when those states are allowed to act collectively they are still bound to respect their shared legal system.

The specificity of the law of integration as a framework that permanently changes the status of the Member States and their relationships is preserved to a large extent. In consequence, although the phenomenon of international agreements among groups of Member States might not be Union law *stricto sensu*, it is not totally foreign to and autonomous from it. One could even see it as bordering with Union law or as a 'mutation' thereof, as *mutant Union law*, complementing the Union framework as a *sui generis* instrument.

The safeguards found in *Pringle* should be read in the light of the clear statement in Opinion 2/13 to the effect that 'the Member States have, by reason of their membership of the [Union], accepted that relationships between them as regards matters covered by the transfer of powers from the Member States to the [Union], *are governed by [Union] law to the exclusion, if [Union] law so requires, of any other law*'.[36] Union law is not just like any other law that the Member States may want to use to frame their interaction. It has a fundamental nature and a priority over any other source of law, including international law. It itself defines the boundaries of the retained powers of the

[36] Opinion 2/13, chapter 6, note 1, at para. 193 (emphasis added).

Member States, and it may require them to use their shared system of law to the exclusion of other systems.

This understanding is confirmed by the judgment in *Achmea*, where its consequences become tangible. In this decision, the Court of Justice recalled the main characteristics of the law of integration, underlining its direct effect, its primacy, and its autonomy from national and international law. On that basis, it held that Article 267 TFEU (on the preliminary rulings procedure) and Article 344 TFEU (prohibiting Member States from submitting disputes concerning Union law to methods of settlement other than those provided in the Treaties), as reflections of the fundamental principle of autonomy of Union law, preclude the arbitration clauses contained in bilateral investment treaties between Member States. By allowing private investors from one Member State to bring disputes against another Member State before an arbitration tribunal, those clauses would 'remove from the jurisdiction of their own courts', and hence from the preliminary rulings mechanism, disputes which may concern the application or interpretation of Union law.[37]

In this context, the general expectation of the Court and of other actors which remain committed to integration is that *inter se* agreements are only provisional arrangements and that in due time those instruments will be repealed and/or repatriated into the Union system, with the adaptations that will be required to respect Union law. In the meantime, the Court tries to contain the damage to the institutional system and to protect the integrity of Union law as much as possible, through limitations on scope and substance. The perception of the Member States of being able to escape from Union law—of being at liberty to escape the Union system—may therefore be no more than an illusion.

It should however be noted that the consequences of this view for legal and institutional practice will depend on the subsequent behaviour of the political institutions and of the Member States, which may respect the thrust of the judgment or may try to play around its edges to enlarge the scope of this phenomenon.

[37] *Achmea*, supra note 7, paras. 32 to 37, 55, and 60.

The recent Commission proposals to integrate the substance of the Fiscal Compact and the European Stability Mechanism into the Union legal framework are an important test case.[38] The first one does not seem to raise fundamental legal issues. While there is much to commend the second one, its assessment can only be ambivalent. On the one hand, the proposal has clear advantages in legal terms, as it would anchor the stability mechanism within the Union legal and institutional system, subjecting its decisions to review by the Court of Justice and to the Charter, and requiring Council approval for the most relevant decisions. On the other hand, the draft Regulation remains very close to the terms of the Treaty establishing the European Stability Mechanism and keeps almost intact its governance structure and decision-making procedures, which might raise issues from the point of view of the institutional balance of the Union and could lead to deadlocks in view of the lighter majorities required for Council approval. Besides, the parallel consent of the euro area Member States to the transfer of the capital to the new Union body is required for the Regulation to be effective. One may thus wonder whether the adaptations introduced would be sufficient to achieve the desired improvements in the effectiveness and European legitimacy of the stability mechanism.

It is uncertain, as this book goes to press, whether even these rather modest proposals will be followed by the Union legislature. Their fate will tell us whether the Union system may reabsorb intergovernmental solutions without being undermined by them, or whether those solutions are a permanent or even growing element of the legal and institutional landscape, altering the balance and structure of the mobile of integration. In other words, only time will tell us whether the risks of the limited 'opening plus framing' the Court felt bound to concede in *Pringle* were compensated by its overall benefits, or whether the Court's resistance was vain and it was Union law that was

[38] Proposal for a Council Directive laying down provisions for strengthening fiscal responsibility and the medium-term budgetary orientation in the Member States (COM(2017) 824, of 6 December 2017); for the proposal on the European Stability Mechanism, see *supra* note 11.

'framed' by the Member States in another episode of the process of erosion of the law of integration.

7

Let me conclude this chapter with a final reflection on the strange 'dissociation disorder' that seems to get hold of the European Council and of the Council at some sensitive junctures, leading to the 'switching of hats' and to the conclusion of international agreements among the representatives of the Member States. This tendency towards dissociation is also connected to the waning of historical consciousness and of solidarity among the Member States. They seem to have forgotten the reasons behind integration. One could even have the impression that some have never been aware of them.

In some of these cases, the Council adopts a Union instrument and immediately afterwards, 'in the margins' of the same Council meeting, its members 'change hats' to meet as an intergovernmental conference, purportedly outside Union law, and adopt an international law instrument that contains fundamental parts of the new mechanism. This hybrid system usually splits a Commission proposal for a Union instrument into two parts: a Union act and an international act. In other cases, only an international act is adopted, as happened with the agreement in simplified form of the defunct 'new settlement' for the UK.[39]

From an institutional perspective, the ease with which the Member States pretend to dissociate themselves from the Union to act outside it gives serious cause for concern. The practice is old, certainly, but in more orthodox times it only concerned matters falling outside the scope of Community law, where it is clear that the Member States can adopt such complementary acts among themselves. Now this tendency has reached areas in which a Union competence could be asserted.

One therapy for this dissociation disorder seems to be the exercise of framing and taming that the Court undertook in

[39] See chapter 5, note 80.

Pringle, but an additional effort towards legal requalification could be possible in some cases. Only the acts of the heads of government or the ministers sitting in the Council which are truly outside the scope of Union law could be considered as being 'outside' the Union system—even if framed by it. In contrast, those acts that fall within the scope of Union law could be requalified as acts of the European Council or of the Council, with all the ensuing legal consequences, including full judicial review before the Court of Justice.[40]

A case in point is the UK's 'new settlement'. In it, the heads of state and government were formally acting as an intergovernmental conference, outside the Union legal order. On close inspection, nonetheless, the act directly concerned Union law in force, interfering with primary law (on subsidiarity) and with the legislative process (on the free movement of workers and citizens) in ways that seem to be incompatible with substantive Union law and to exceed the limited powers of the European Council, thus encroaching upon the institutional balance.[41] Since this defunct act could have been requalified as a measure of the European Council in view of its substance, all the avenues to review its legality vis-à-vis Union law and to preserve the autonomy of the latter would have been open.

[40] See the *ERTA* judgment, see chapter 1, note 1, at paras. 52 and 53.

[41] On the limited powers of the European Council vis-à-vis the Commission and the Council, see Joined Cases C-643/15 and C-647/15, *Slovakia and Hungary v. Council*, EU:C:2017:631, at paras. 145–49.

8

CONCLUDING THOUGHTS

One of the traits that distinguishes Union law from the laws of the Member States is its constant dynamism—its open and creative character. This makes it fascinating, but also gives the impression that it is condemned to be always under construction and to have a precarious mode of being. It appears as if it could never stop being a sort of nomadic law, without fixed abode, always in flux, sometimes growing, sometimes shrinking, and at the risk of disintegrating at great speed, like those buildings that one sees today and tomorrow are no more, leaving an eerie empty space.

The grave crisis that has been haunting the Union at many levels for so long, and which is far from being over, has exposed even more the fragility of the European construction, and among all its elements the impermanence of its law, which many see as an obnoxious remnant from the past—an obstacle that prevents the Member States from returning to the dubious paradise of unfettered sovereignty.

Much is left of it, and what remains seems to be in good shape. But it is subject to so much pressure, torn by so many contradictions and complexities, that it sometimes appears as if it could collapse at any time. The spirit which conceived it and which has sustained it throughout the decades seems not to have much currency at present, and no adequate replacement has been found. This explains all the pressures exerted to transform integration and its law into a more flexible framework of cooperation, if not to do away with it.

Many have the impression that we live in catastrophic times. In our rather modest theme, which is no more than a tiny piece of the human jigsaw, melancholy takes hold of us when we see how the promising mobile of the 1950s is gradually drifting away from its noble initial objectives. One could think that it is no longer the solid and coherent structure that the drafters

What's Left of the Law of Integration? Decay and Resistance in European Union Law.
First Edition. Julio Baquero Cruz. Published 2018 by Oxford University Press.

conceived, but, with Walter Benjamin, just a thin patina whose fate is to be thrown away in the heap of ruins that we call history.

The reality of decay is undeniable, and it reveals something. Besides the pressure to change the very notion of integration, weakening it, there is pressure to change its law, transforming it into a mere instrument at the service of the political process. This book has analysed some examples of this phenomenon, but there are others. There is also some resistance against that pressure, but in the long run the law of integration may only survive under certain conditions.

The first, to which I have already referred several times, is that the Member States and Union citizens must share a broad consensus about the foundations of European integration. Integration and its law cannot subsist if they host states and peoples that have incompatible conceptions of the Union and of the consequences it has for them. In the long term, that fundamental disagreement can only bring decay and disintegration. In the medium term, if the views do not converge, it inevitably leads to a very hard choice between an enlarged Union which is fragmented, incoherent, and weakened by problems that it cannot resolve, and a somewhat smaller but perhaps more solid Union. There is an optimal point at which the curves of widening and deepening cross. To get closer to it, preferably through a recovery of that broad consensus, is a vital task for the future of integration.

The second condition is that the Union should always act in the European general interest, and not to advance the interests of this or that country or group of countries, and even less of particular economic groups. Integration is designed to work against national selfishness and cannot subsist without supranational solidarity. Its essence is subverted if it turns, for whatever reason, into a mechanism of domination that permanently favours certain countries or certain interests, while harming others. At present, the wealth generated by the Union does not seem to be distributed in a fair manner, be it between or within the states. There are winners and losers in any polity, but being together should benefit everybody in the long run. The crisis, however, has led to a fierce fight to reduce the costs and maintain or even increase the benefits of integration, thwarting the basic principle of solidarity and stirring old nationalist tendencies. In this respect we also seem to be far from the optimal point in the equation of the costs and benefits of integration.

This leads us to the third condition: sufficient legitimacy. The obstacles that sometimes prevent the Union from acting in the European general interest produce a deficit in output legitimacy that the current structure does not seem to be able to correct. The long-term subsistence of integration and its law requires an improvement of its political process, in general and also in the most problematic sectors, such as economic and monetary union, to ensure that it always works in the European general interest and not for the benefit of particular interests. This improvement is a difficult matter. The political system of the Union is a fragile machine reflecting a very delicate balance achieved through the decades. In view of the social and cultural conditions of the Union, the kind of democracy that it may have is not the standard one of a nation state. Even so, gradual improvements are possible and desirable. They could lead to a better functioning of the Union for the benefit of all Europeans.

Finally, integration and its law cannot subsist without European citizens, including European lawyers who know it and care about it. In both respects the situation is far from perfect. One is tempted to go around with a lamp while the sun is up in the sky, like Diogenes, asking: 'Have you seen a European citizen?' or 'Have you seen a European lawyer?' Union citizens are there, with their European status and rights, and often also with their European obligations and burdens, which may be heavy. But they are mostly passive and live in the partial illusion of their national political structures, not always conscious of what the European political process means and does to them. Besides the problems of representation and participation evoked here, that lack of awareness prevents most European citizens from being an active presence in the Union.

There are European jurists, certainly, though mostly in Brussels and Luxembourg—and that's also insufficient. If legal actors in the Member States do not see Union law as a normal part of their daily work, and do not see themselves as European jurists in addition to being national jurists, Union law could never work the way it should, with the significant costs this entails. The crisis has not improved things. The general impression is that of a national revival, which has also been seen in the world of law.

One of the last times I saw Pierre Pescatore, in 2004, he said something that made me understand that he was a bit disappointed with the generation of Community lawyers that came after his, who had no experience of the war, had been educated in the national legal tradition, and sometimes fiddled with the law of integration in ways that seemed to betray its historical roots and spirit. But he immediately added that he put all his hopes in the coming generations. Indeed, let us hope that they understand better the legacy and dignity of that law, preserving its achievements and perhaps, one day, bringing them to completion in order to form a better Union.

INDEX

Milton Keynes UK
Ingram Content Group UK Ltd.
UKHW020223090923
428331UK00005B/63

9 780198 830610